IN BETWEEN THE SILENCE

In Between the Silence

Roo Stove

To Sam
Who taught me about love

Copyright © 2025 by Roo Stove
All rights reserved. No part of this book may be reproduced in any manner whatsoever without written permission except in the case of brief quotations embodied in critical articles and reviews.
No A.I. was used in the writing of this novel.
First Printing, 2025

1

Chapter 1

Sydney, Australia, has a benign beauty. In its brightness, it looks like a city where nothing can hurt. Glancing... no, not so much glancing as staring trance-like from a window, holding it momentarily on such a day brings on the notion of possible immortality. Or perhaps, an Australian interpretation of *joie de vivre*: believing that, to have an icy glass of beer and a soft cool chair in the shade on a hot day is one of the closest non-spiritual experiences to Utopia that there can be. To really establish a spiritual plain, a bottle of Bundy Rum, the Square Bear might be added, and come evening usually is.

Sydney has an attractiveness, which doesn't always withstand close inspection. In parts, the ugliness underneath seems to allow a discharge of diverse scum to fester up onto the surface. But to delve into a city's darkness and raw wounds would probably be unfair. Perfection is not a human trait.

So we see, it is a Sunday. The pubs and ice-cream parlours are industriously catering to adult and children's addictions. Business is benefiting from the city's light. Customers, as they order the cold refreshments comment on the weather as if it were a new experience. "Bloody hot, eh?" They walk upright and afresh out of air-conditioned buildings and wilt before reaching the next corner. Shops on the beachfronts, and in the side streets nearby, are enjoying the earnings of a warm springtime promise of an enterprise filled summer. Vulture-like sea gulls are relishing this sudden upsurge in tasty morsels of debris.

A Sunday, and non-religious types, those who prefer to take their pietistic

"OK."

"I'll call when the fruit salad's ready."

"Can I change into my swimmers!" the child shouts after her mother. "If you must... Then I suppose I can just hose you down after most of your lunch ends up in your lap."

"What? I mean, I beg your pardon?"

"Nothing. Just talking to myself."

"You're weird."

"Yes. I know sweetheart. Never mind."

2

Chapter 2

One truth arose from the confusion - the child was gone. The mother sat in the police station withdrawn into a horror. A cup of tea, grown tepid down on the floor beside her left foot, rippled in answer to the busy footsteps vibrating the passageway. She thought she would never be able to breathe without pain again.

"Mrs. Brenner?"

"You've found her?" She jumped up, the cup flew sideways and a small stream of tea snaked an uneven track over the well-worn linoleum.

"No. I'm sorry. Constable Moller! Could you clean this up? Come with me Mrs. Brenner. It's a little quieter in an interview room. I'll get you another cup of... coffee, was it?"

"No."

"Tea then."

"No. I mean, no thank you. I'm not thirsty."

"Are you sure? You've had a bit of a shock."

She gave a smile in response to his kindness but declined the drink. Queasiness too strong... Moreover, the officer was correct, the interview room was somewhat quieter, making a place for her fears to become much louder. Louder to a point near to immersing her completely in a gulf of panic. Deep enough that she feared a drowning.

"Oh, God!"

"Mrs. Brenner? Listen. Take deep breaths. You're hyperventilating. Would you like to see our Medical Officer?"

"No, it's, OK. It's passing. I'm sorry. I'm not usually such..."

"You've had a shit... an appalling afternoon. Now what we have to do is work out a direction to go. Do you know of anyone who would take your daughter? For any reason. Friends? Your husband?"

"No. No."

"Can we contact your husband for you now?"

"I don't think so. He's dead."

"Oh," the detective shuffled papers and pushed them aside as if they had given him misleading information. "I'm sorry."

"No. It's OK. He was a bastard."

"Oh... Oh?"

Chapter 3

*T*ime heals all wounds.
   Bullshit.

4

Chapter 4

Fifteen Years Later

The Police Station
Anaesthetises. That's what time does. It covers over wounds like a layer of dust, so that they become harder to see, a little dulled, but they're there just the same. It doesn't take much to reveal them, just a slight breeze or a bump.

"Beth, they may have found Ingrid."

Elizabeth Brenner felt her damage purl. It started near her heart and ended with her legs quaking as if she had just finished running a marathon. 'There's never enough oxygen in the world,' she thought just before she fainted. The black came creeping over her, but she was powerless, no fight left.

Blood returned to her brain as quickly as it had left, Elizabeth rose from her head between her knees position and tried to regain the dignity she felt the faint had removed.

"You said you wouldn't do this again unless you were positive," she told the policeman as he handed her a brandy in a take-away coffee cup.

"Elizabeth, I know you've had false hope before, but this time its real hope. I've seen her... She looks a bit like you... You know there have been advances in forensics since she went missing... DNA printing, the hairbrush from her room... Beth, it's got to be her."

"No. No. Don't do this to me again. Bob. Please."

"You know I wouldn't unless I felt sure..."

* * *

Emergency teams had been called to a property near Peats Ridge in the Mangrove Mountain district, some thirty kilometres from Sydney, after an explosion. Seasoned police officers used salty language and were made subdued by the shock of what they had found.

"Jesus Christ. How..."

When the distilling equipment used in the process of making amphetamines had sparked, the place had ruptured with the force of a group of domino-effected land mines. An arsenal nearby, containing explosives blew with such intensity that pieces of human were found in trees over half a kilometre away. There too, they found the emaciated young woman, shackled to a tree, with a noticeable piece of shrapnel sticking out of her side, and blood seeping ground-ward. A projectiled triangle of metal, that would have felled a horse, in her, but she appeared oblivious to the wound and the tin protuberance. Unaware of the police also, until one of them touched her on the shoulder. Terrified, she scrambled as far away as shackles, chain, and the extrusive scraping metal in her side would allow.

"Jesus Christ!"

They'd had to wait for the ambulance to bounce its way frenetically to them through the severe bush land. Once there, it took three police to hold the woman down. Once the effects of the needle hit and it hit hard and sudden they could tend to physical wounds. For some time, the emergency service personnel worked on the tranquillised woman. Their voices cracking in disgust and anger.

"This shackle has been around her ankle for so long, the skin's started to grow over the metal! They're going to have to cut the bloody thing off in surgery. What's been going on here?"

Some questions can never be answered. Some questions should never be answered. And some demand an answer.

In the hospital, chemical restraint was administered again after surgery. As soon as she had regained full consciousness the woman's flight responses reactivated. She was sedated again, then moved from the recovery ward directly to the psychiatric unit over the road from the hospital proper, where it was thought the staff were more equipped to cope with the woman's obvious trauma and agitation.

Confused and worn, Jane Doe woke again in new surroundings, afraid. This time she was in bed in the High Dependency Area of the unit, and the police guard had been relieved of their duty. It would take manic strength to escape, and the patient was overcome by a postoperative fatigue that acted as an extra confinement.

* * *

Elizabeth Brenner, for the first time in fifteen years, was about to feel optimism. She faced the policeman, put her brandy down on his desk and asked, "Do you really think it's her, Bob?"

The policeman gulped his drink in one swallow.

5

Chapter 5

"Ingrid?"

The woman did not respond. Elizabeth hesitated, surrounded by her expectations and on hold dreams that were rattling the gates of freedom, eager to plan this new future.

Sometimes words fall from a mouth, even the mouths of shy, reticent people, without prior notice to the speaker. They plunge like a bungee jumper who's neglected to attach their leg strap and it's not until the fall has started that they sense that perhaps they've forgotten something, and all that they have now are consequences.

"It's Mum," Elizabeth said without warning even herself.

Blasts of heat burnt through the barrier of non-existence. 'It's Mum,' the voice had said, and I flinched with the lies of it all. She is dead. My mother had always been dead. They lock me up, like always, but say they don't want to hurt me. And now more lies.

"Jeez, if looks could kill," a nurse muttered, seeing for the first time, a light in the eyes of their patient as she reacted to Mrs. Brenner. But the look disappeared as quickly as it came and they were left with nothing.

Liz, her maternal instinct reawakening, continued, grasping hope, and the belief that any reaction was a sign. A promise filled sign.

"It's so good to see you again. You don't know how long I've waited... We... I... There's been... Oh, Ingrid."

She weeps over me, this woman; the bitch whose first words are lies. Sleep. Let me sleep. Elizabeth left the sleeping woman/child, left the room, the ward, the hospital, feeling wounded but not sure why. She ignored her car in the car park and walked. North, south, east, west, sometimes direction had no direction. She stood for some moments on the bridge that spanned the railway tracks, watching, hearing as a train shrieked its electrical progress beneath her and vibrated her nerves into a different pattern.

"Fuck you," she said to no one in particular, just feeling the tip of anger that had lived with her longer than her own child.

There was a pub on the other side of the railway station. It didn't look discouraging. There were no subtle, or overt, signs of male only zones or angry looking people by the pool tables. Elizabeth intruded. The music was gentle and none too old and the patrons seemed at home and nicely indifferent to the entrance of a lone female.

"Vodka and orange, please."

Elizabeth found a table in the unpeopled outdoor courtyard where a rather imprisoned looking cockatoo resided in a cage, hounded by small sparrows that oozed freedom as they flew in and out of the trapped one's cage, helping themselves to its food.

"I could let you go," said Elizabeth to the confined animal, "But you wouldn't last a minute."

Not that she had little faith in the bird; it was the world that had left Elizabeth without trust. It contained a cruelty, an ingrained biting hardness that civilisation could or would never seem able to soften. Elizabeth moved over to the cage, holding her drink and the small sparrows fled her size.

"Are you all right?" she asked the cockatoo, and it hissed with a savage anger at her. "Well fuck you, too!" she replied, and returned to the seat she had chosen feeling self pity chew at her sense of worth. Tears slid to the surface so Elizabeth swallowed them back with a gulp of vodka.

As it approached lunchtime the courtyard populated somewhat, speckling with an odd assortment of suits and ties, next to singlets and shorts. Most of the women wore those floral numbers favoured by banks and real estate offices. Elizabeth was glad her chosen seat was made isolated by a large fern, which stretched about her like a private bower sheltering her from sociable advances, while she became slowly, and surely smashed.

It was here, inebriated, alone amongst the ferns that Senior Detective Robert Porter found Elizabeth, some two hours later.

"Ah ha. There you are. I'll be back in a minute." He returned as predicted, carrying a schooner of beer and vodka and orange for Elizabeth.

"Good detective work. How'd you find me?"

"Process of elimination. Saw your car first. Tried the ward, next the hospital coffee shop. Then here."

"Am I that predictable?"

"No. I am. You did exactly what I did, after seeing Ingrid for the first time."

"Oh, Jesus, Bob." Alcohol and grief merged within Elizabeth and she began to cry, noiselessly, but with much water. Robert held her hand without talk until the jag ended.

"Thank you," Elizabeth said, before taking a swig of her neglected drink. "What for?"

"For not doing that, 'don't cry, let me fix everything' thing that men sometimes do."

"Hey, I've been a cop long enough to know to let people cry when they can. What about you? When was the last time you ate? I'm going to order us some food and see if I can't catch up a little with your state of inebriation."

"Are you saying I'm drunk?"

"As a nit."

Soon, there slipped a happy dereliction into the atmosphere. Perhaps alcohol induced, perhaps not. They ate; they drank, and watched the night reach toward them, without thought of work, duty, or tomorrow.

"I've booked a room upstairs, can't get back to Sydney in this condition," said Bob, after he'd downed several scotches. "Do you want to share?"

There was a sobering moment for Liz, with this idea of being human. She felt as if she had dropped or made redundant pieces of her personality as each sadness, from the time of Ingrid's disappearance and on, hit. Chiselling off jagged edges until only the bits needed for the barest survival remained. With each day and long night it appeared necessary for Liz to deny entry to emotions, or she would become unexpectedly and uncomfortably aware of her own potential for implosion. Robert, she allowed, listening to her near atrophied inner exponent of appraisal, was not an unattractive man. Age and experience showed the signs of passage and arrival but had not completely stolen traces of his youth.

"No strings," he added. "Just sleep."

"I don't know. Strings may not be so bad," Liz said, surprising herself. "Sorry. You're right. I've had too much to drink. It's been a bloody weird day."

"Let's just get a brandy, for the ro... stairs, and see. I'll be back," he promised, and moved quickly toward the bar, wishing perhaps to hide or run from embarrassment under the protection of decisive action. Were rules meant to be broken?

Liz sat, watching the night insects hover about the beer garden lighting, willing herself to sober, and not sure if she really wanted to.

6

Chapter 6

She woke screaming.
***

7

Chapter 7

Night staff gave way to day. Days bled into weeks. Every morning, like this morning, the noise of the ward grew busy. A smell somewhere between cooking toast and "fire!" wafted through from the kitchen, with a freedom to go anywhere, triggering the appetites of some patients and staving the hunger of others. Those of the ward who could, sat at the table as a nurse wheeled in the breakfast trolley, negotiating the locked door with an electronic keycard and an under the breath curse as shin met metal.

Ingrid remained confined in her bed.

"Good morning. You must be hungry. I've bought you some toast and juice. Or there's cereal. Anyway..."

She is aware. Her eyes are following me.

"I can help you sit up. You realise your leg is very sore and needs to be kept still. If you're OK I'll help sit up. Do you understand?"

No. She's gone again. No, no, there's a nod. She's here.

"Let me just put this tray down. OK. You're doing really well this morning. Let's get you sitting up. You all right? Not dizzy?"

A barely perceptible shake of the head. Understanding. Breakthrough? But Ingrid was again under sedation by the time Elizabeth arrived.

"She's had a good morning. Even ate breakfast. But then she had some sort of episode, we don't know, flashback or a severe anxiety attack."

"Is she alright?"

"She's ripped open her leg a bit. The doctor's checked it and said it shouldn't postpone the graft. She's still on antibiotics, so infection shouldn't be a worry. Honestly she's doing better."

"I can see her?"

"Sure. She's had some medication earlier so if you can get her to drink something it'd be good. We don't want her back on a drip if we can help it. Come on in."

Elizabeth felt what was becoming a familiar sense of foreboding when the nurse opened the door to the High Dependency Area. She wished she didn't but she felt relieved when she realised most of the patients had gone outside with a nurse to get some fresh air.

"Your Mum's here, Ingrid."

There was the hostile look.

"What's wrong?" Elizabeth asked, as the nurse left. "You seem angry at me. Have I done something wrong?"

No reaction.

"Oh, I think I see. Do you think that maybe I'm not your mother? Is that it? Yes?" Elizabeth noticed a slight movement that she read as interest. "Because if it is, I have a piece of paper here." She fumbled into her handbag. "See, they took your blood and some of mine. It says right here that it is 99.9 percent positive that I'm your mother." Elizabeth laid the paper on Ingrid's chest. "So you see, kiddo, I'm your mother whether you like it or not." God, this hangover wasn't helping.

"Dead," Ingrid said. Her first word.

"Did you say 'dead'? Dead? What... did you think I was dead? Did they tell you I was dead? Ingrid? Shit. Nurse!"

Stop calling for your mother, little bitch. Your mother's dead that's why you're with me. She left you to me. Wasn't that nice of her, eh? You're mine.

"She'll probably sleep a while now. Are you all right, Mrs. Brenner?"

"I... I really don't know. I think I'll go for a walk and come back later this afternoon. I'm a bit..."

"OK. She's under our care, so if you want to rest, have time to yourself, don't worry, she'll be looked after."

"I've had fifteen years to myself... I'll come back later. Can you let me out?" "Sure." The nurse opened the three sets of electronically controlled doors to allow Elizabeth outside. The light of day seemed extra bright. Painful.

Walking up the nearby steps toward street level, Elizabeth felt a tiredness that she knew had nothing to do with lack of sleep. A lack, possibly. There is an overload, a point where a person has more thoughts and feelings than they can deal with at one time but no place to put the excess. One could walk around in small circles screaming or do as Elizabeth did and walk to the nearest coffee shop. There are probably other choices but stress and lack of finances can be limiting. A trip to the Caribbean was pretty much out of the question.

"Can I have a Jamaican blend coffee, please?"

Sometimes, there is compromise. Tiny, minute mercies.

Elizabeth took a seat at a table in front of the huge glass window that overlooked the main street and the railway station. Contemplated the pile of newspapers for patrons to peruse and decided her brain was full enough.

"Your coffee."

"Thank you."

"And I think your handbag is ringing."

"Sorry? Oh. Yes, it's my mobile."

She quickly pulled the phone from her bag and glanced at the screen; saw that it was her office.

"Hello? Yes, hi, Darren. I'm sorry. I'll be back tomorrow. I will have to arrange for some extended leave. I beg your pardon. Just a minute, you what? I think I'm entitled to a little more... Sorry? You know what, go to Hell. You are a piece of..."

She pressed the red hang up symbol on her phone, cutting off the call. Tapping a button was not quite as satisfying as slamming down a telephone. Elizabeth laughed aloud, not sure if there was a note of hysteria slipping in or out. She wanted to tell the couple at the table next to her that she had just been fired but controlled the urge. Etiquettly speaking it would probably be a cafe faux pas. *Hated that job anyway.* She was both relieved and frightened at the sudden unemployment. Knew that she could fight the unfair dismissal but didn't think she cared enough. Elizabeth hoped they deposited what they owed into her account so that she didn't have deal with the firm ever again.

The phone rang again; she saw that it was the work number and sent the call straight to Voice Mail. 'If you're only young once, how many times are you old?' Elizabeth wondered, feeling that tiredness again. She signalled for another cup of coffee.

This cup she enjoyed without interruption, able to look out of the window and watch people going about their lives while keeping her mind blank enough not to think about her own. But reality has the right of infringement, and it pushed its way back the moment Elizabeth placed her cup on the saucer for the final time. Because she was now jobless there was felt a great undeniable need to spend money. She paid the bill at the counter and headed for the shopping centre proper. In *Best and Less* she purchased a nightie, some underwear, a pair of jeans, T-shirt and a jumper for Ingrid. In *Woolworth's* - toiletries.

Later, with a kebab in hand, and finding the food court too noisy Elizabeth fled the building, saw a park across the road and settled for a bench near the fountain. Or what should have been a fountain. The water was not running, the unused pipes looked bored in their inactivity, pretending to be a sculpture but only managing abandoned scrap. It was pleasant enough for a fast lunch. Pigeons dodged about searching for food remnants, and people sat about flicking crumbs their way. The birds zeroed in on Elizabeth, as if they were smart enough to know. She was a sucker. A born-again sucker. Bits fell from her wrapper and the pigeons found their disappointment almost more palatable than the lettuce and looked at Elizabeth as if she could do better. Of course she could. She threw down a piece of flat bread and there became a flutter. Feathers flew, mostly with birds attached. One tan and white pigeon landed with what seemed to be a sense of possession on Elizabeth's knee. She hand fed it a piece of bread. Next, a portion of chicken.

"Cannibal," she said, as the pigeon swallowed without concern the piece of flesh and skittered about on Elizabeth's knee waiting for the next scrap. The bird scratched a little as it slid but Elizabeth was somewhat beyond feeling.

"Dead and fired on the same day. Enjoy this while you can," Elizabeth told the bird, feeding it more bread. "I'm not really here." She sighed, "I'm not really anything."

Perhaps a shred of melancholy had infiltrated Elizabeth's demeanour.

Elizabeth did not feel at all mother-like. She felt defrauded and disliked herself for feeling so. Illogically she had expected, in moments of periodic optimism that she would get Ingrid back in the same condition as the child had been when she disappeared. Yes, she'd expected Ingrid, if she was alive to have matured, but not into this... wound, this frightened living reaction to God knows what. A child is a canvas with a basic etching already there. Life experience adds the colour, depth and a persistence of personality. But what happens to those who are denied the chance to soak in the shades of biography? Are they forever blinded to the colour of now and remain in the grey of loss. Ingrid appeared to be a direct response to deprivation; a reaction so ingrained into her canvas that it would be difficult to add life with its generous colour or erase the blackness of the trauma she had endured.

"Can you spare a dollar?"

"What? Yes. I suppose," answered Elizabeth, looking up to see a skinny, ravaged faced woman of about thirty, who smiled the tooth-missing smile of the enduring poor. "Although I might be asking you next week." Elizabeth added pulling a gold coin from her purse and handing it to the woman.

"Thanks. I'm dying for a coffee."

The woman moved off and approached other lunchers for spare change.

"Piss off, I work hard for my money," said one man, punctuating with a self-inflating snarl. The life worn woman shrugged and moved on.

Elizabeth rose, causing a stir among the pigeons. She brushed crumbs from her lap and picked up her shopping. Spun slightly to get her bearings and headed towards the main road. She walked past the pub feeling only a slight pull to the front door. She was now, officially, on a limited budget. Best to buy alcohol from the outlets, no more sitting in a bar paying twice the price for the privilege of drinking from a glass when she could sit quite comfortably in a wardrobe and drink straight from the bottle.

8

Chapter 8

Speaking into the intercom of the clinic had begun to lose its fear factor.

"Mrs Brenner for Ingrid," Elizabeth announced with a confidence that she didn't quite feel on the inside but was ready to portray on the surface.

"Beg your pardon?" cackled the intercom in return, and Elizabeth felt her aplomb splutter like a doused candle.

"Eliz... Elizabeth... Elizabeth Brenner," she stuttered. "To see Ingrid."

The door buzzed and Elizabeth passed through and waited at the next glass doors to be let in.

"Hello Mrs Brenner," the nurse said as he opened the door. "Been shopping?"

"Hmm. Yes. Some things I thought Ingrid might need."

"I'm sorry but I'll have to go through them."

"That's OK. But can I just take the bomb out first, it feels suddenly inappropriate."

"What?"

"Sorry. Gallows humour. Stupid things just slip out when I least expect them," Elizabeth apologised. "You ought to hear me at funerals, I find myself almost doing stand-up..."

"This is OK. You can come through," said the nurse efficiently and Elizabeth shut up, and allowed herself to be guided into the High Dependency Area.

"No. Stop! Let me out again. I forgot something. Can I leave these bags here?"

The nurse looked a little confused but took the bags. Elizabeth waited impatiently for the door opening processes to be completed in the wretchedly slow motion that seems reserved by kismet for those in haste. Finally, she was emancipated. There was an almost sprint up the stairs to street level until her body reminded her how old she was, and she slowed down to an oldster's fast pace, regaining her breath, except maybe for a slight wheeze.

"It's a meat pie. Do you remember? It's what you wanted for lunch... that day."

Ingrid raised an eyebrow and Elizabeth could see her 'dead mother' conviction falter. 'Ah, she remembers something... but don't rush her.'

"Eat it while it's still tepid," said Elizabeth of the pie.

"Can I micro-wave that for you, Mrs Brenner?" asked a nurse stopping at the cubicle entrance.

"No," whispered Ingrid and reached for the pie.

Elizabeth handed over the pie but instead of unwrapping it to eat Ingrid stashed it under her pillow.

"You don't need to do that, Ingrid," protested the nurse. "If you don't want to eat it yet, we can heat it up later. No one will take it from you. If you like we can keep it in the fridge till you want to eat it."

"No."

"Well, at least put it on the bedside table. You really don't want to squash that under your pillow."

"Certainly not without added flavouring," Elizabeth said, handing Ingrid the sachet of tomato sauce she'd been holding.

Ingrid smiled more-or-less in Elizabeth's direction and then carefully placed the pie and sauce in the bedside table drawer. The nurse left the cubicle when the sound of an argument between other patients became overheated in the television area.

"I thought she'd never leave," said Elizabeth, then lapsed into silence. She didn't really know what to say now. "How about this weather… I've been thinking. Now that I haven't got a job… and um, I don't need the Sydney flat anymore. I was always scared to leave it in case you found your way home…"

This time her voice trailed off in to tears as she realised she could put away the searching, and the waiting. All those young girls, whom at first glance were Ingrid and at second glance, were not. All the times the phone had stopped ringing seconds before she'd reached it, when she had thrown herself in a rugby type tackle at it only to hear the tortuous 'beep' of the dial tone. The instances she thought she'd heard knocks on the door while she was in the shower and had rushed out with shampoo in her hair and a towel hanging about her, only to find an empty hall. Her over alertness had become second nature and now… now she could relax.

"Aggh!" yelped Ingrid in the quiet way of those afraid of noise, and the look, or lack of look in her eyes told Elizabeth she was somewhere else.

"Nurse!" called Elizabeth, feeling quite a way from relaxed.

She knew better now than to try and touch Ingrid, but she wanted to take her child into her arms and place protective arms around her. The nurse took a look at Ingrid.

"Do you think you can persuade her to take some Valium syrup?"

"Sure," answered Elizabeth weakly. "If she won't take it, I will… It's OK, sweetie. The nurse will be back with something that will make you feel better. Don't hurt yourself. Please."

Ingrid began to rock, her bandaged leg drawn towards her, in a strong effort to soothe herself. Elizabeth could do nothing but perceive her own impotence.

You will not eat until I say you can. The next time you scratch me; there'll be more consequences than just no food. Look. Look at the blood on my fucking new shirt! You can forget about fucking food all together, you fucking little cow.

"Can I get you a cup of tea or coffee Mrs Brenner?" asked the nurse forcing Elizabeth from the vacuum she'd fallen or retreated into.

Ingrid was still asleep.

"Sure. Coffee would be fine. White with two, please."

The nurse left and Elizabeth stared at her daughter. Her Ingrid, asleep, alone, unfamiliar. The bond that had been so tenable had been ripped in such a painful way that Liz was unsure if she'd ever get back that mother/daughter thing they'd had. 'Don't feel I even know this woman, let alone feel related to her,' she thought and felt instant guilt for doing so. Fifteen important years when it came to children. Elizabeth herself had not grown over the years, except perhaps outward in a middle-aged spreading kind of way, but Ingrid? These had been the developing years, the child to woman years. Not repeatable in any way. There had been milestones missed for Ingrid. Rites of passage unattended. Wronged by captivity, Ingrid knew nothing of the world unchained, nor her place in it.

"There you are, Mrs Brenner. 2SM."

Elizabeth took the offered coffee and slipped quickly back into preoccupation. Where to start? Had Ingrid been near a school? Unlikely. Did she still have the rudimentary skills that enabled survival in society? Did she know how to apply mascara? 'Shut up.' Elizabeth told herself. She looked again at the sleeping woman and was sure she could see traces of her ancestry in Ingrid's bone structure. *She must be Ingrid. Who else could she be?*

Her child stirred, groaned a little, and began the painful process of surfacing.

"Hi," said Elizabeth softly, so as not to make the awakening harsh.

"Mm," she answered, speech still beyond. The heaviness of the sedation pushing.

"You're probably dry, have a sip of this water."

Elizabeth swapped her coffee for water and held the cup and straw to Ingrid, she sipped.

"Thadda girl," she said, automatically dredging the patter from deep within their shared past. She could tell Ingrid felt uncomfortable with closeness, so stretched her arm and kept her body back. "I guess you'll get used to me in time," she murmured. "So anyway, as I was saying, if I sell the unit in Bondi I should have plenty of money for a villa or something around here, and maybe six months off. I think I deserve that anyway. Should've been having long service time anyhow... Those bastards. Still... That way I can be with you and you can have the treatment you need on your leg and here... I've a friend who lives in Tascott, not far from here. She might let me stay there till it's all sorted. What do you think?

"Pie."

"OK. That's what I was hoping you'd say. Do you want me to get it heated for you?"

Liz reached into the bedside table for the meat pie and felt strangely elated. Not strange as in odd, but as in remarkable. It had been a long time since she'd felt anything even approaching elation.

9

Chapter 9
Liz

I decided to walk to the hospital. A one-way trip was about four kilometres of mostly waterside tramping. The morning was light and temperate and as I walked the heat seeped into me and I stepped straight into a better mood.

I heard a shriek of protest from a sea gull, and traffic, a mechanical crane, road

works - sounds fading in and out, like the noise was alive and breathing.

The footpath on my street guided me straight downhill to the main road. There the path joined a shared pedestrian/bike way that twisted gently along the waterside and led eventually to the CBD. I headed down the hill toward the harbour, the view of the water made me sigh; as I breathed in a kind of visual tonic. Even an abandoned waterside restaurant, with its de-evolution into paint-peeling shabbiness, looked worthy of a postcard. The local ferry, stretched out at the yachting marina in front of the waking harbour back-drop, was taking on the first post-commuter passengers of the day. I was the only pedestrian on the path for some minutes and when the traffic waned momentarily, it seemed a big quiet. There was a kind of post-apocalyptic feel for a second. Then the traffic noise built up again and a man with a black Labrador strode past me.

Outside the waterside fish and ship shop with its 'closed' sign on the door, seagulls gathered, waiting for opening hours, among them, one pigeon. It was funny how there always seemed to be one random other bird in a seagull cluster. As I passed, a fight broke out amongst them as they zeroed in on some piece of edible detritus. It was a loud contest with the winner gulping down whatever the prize was in one swallow.

"Way to savour your food,' I told the victorious bird as I moved by.

After minutes of easy walking, I came to the verge of a roundabout, where a left rum would take me up over a railway bridge and to the hospital side of town, someone yelled, 'hey, darlin', from a car window. I turned to see if there was anybody behind me but I was still alone. 'Well,' I thought, not knowing whether to accept it as a complement or bristle in a feminist kind of way. My step faltered and there was a second of regaining my pace. "Smooth, Liz, I said out aloud.

At the top of the hill, which was an almost heart attack inducing incline, sat the hospital. As I approached, panting somewhat, I felt myself flinch inward, in preparation for entry into the psychiatric ward. Inside, it was oppressive, as if anger was trapped seething in all of the corners, ready to rage against imprisonment. I knew I would ride the bus home, depleted.

"Fuck off! You fucking turd!"

"Suzie!" a nurse cried.

"She pulled my nicotine patch on and stuck it on herself. The stupid fucking bitch," continued Suzie.

I edged past the nurse and the fuming woman to and move outside to wait for Ingrid.

"Here we are, Liz." A nurse herded Ingrid toward me. "The doctor wants to see you as soon as he can get away."

"Okay."

Ingrid, hunched in the demeanour of the wounded, slid into the chair next to me, dropping her crutches. She made no effort at communication.

"Hi, sweetie."

I was now used to Ingrid's small signs of communication. It wasn't a reluctance to impart her news or views, Ingrid appeared afraid and

I wasn't sure how to allay these fears and hoped time would take care of them in that comfy blanket way it sometimes had.

Ingrid gave a weak grin, her way of answering and letting me know she was there.

"How are you feeling? I thought we might go out for some real coffee." The unit only served up a tasteless decaffeinated coffee, hard on the taste buds but, from the patient's point of view, better than nothing. "If you're up to it?" Ingrid made a reach for her crutches, "Not yet," I said, "We have to see the doctor first."
The doctor was blunt.

"We need the room and you need to decide whether to send Ingrid to rehab or just take her home. We have done all we can here. We've finished with the surgery. It's just emotional and physical healing from here."

"Oh," I said.

"She does have complex post-traumatic stress disorder and a mood disorder, but she really isn't dysfunctional enough to warrant staying in a mental health unit. It's probably more distressing for her than helpful."

"Oh, okay," I managed to say through my fear. I was afraid I wasn't ready. I was afraid Ingrid wasn't ready. "But she's so..."

"Home," said Ingrid.

"She can go to rehab," the doctor continued. "But there are no beds locally and
there are more severely brain damaged people that need them when they become
available, unless you're able to go private?"

"No. No. I've only just bought a house here on the coast. I... I..."
"Home."

"I've taken the liberty of writing you a referral to a local psychiatrist. She's a good

"I've taken the liberty of writing you a referral to a local psychiatrist. She's a good behavioural therapist and has done a lot of work with post-traumatic stress disorder. You've an appointment for Wednesday, ten o'clock... I had her slip you to the top of her waiting list; it's usually three months to wait."

The doctor handed Liz an envelope.

"Thank you. I guess home it is," Liz said a little unsurely.

"No rush. Take a couple of days to prepare."

"Home," pitched Ingrid.

Liz pushed back in her chair weighted by events. She stole a look at her child. "Might as well make it today, Ingrid seems keen to get out of here."

"Yes," Ingrid agreed, animated by enthusiasm.

"Are you sure?" the doctor asked, concerned by the haste he had initiated.

"I think Ingrid has been locked up for long enough."

"I wouldn't call..."

"Sorry, but you know what I mean... Now, what do I need to know about medication?"

There was so little to pack for Ingrid. So little of life in a bag. Liz's fear would have needed a suitcase twice the size to bear it away, if she were to let it out of her skin.

"How are you feeling?" she asked her daughter as they waited for a taxi, a sense of looking for empathy. "Scared?"

Ingrid shook her head and quietly said, "No."

"I am," Liz admitted.

10

Chapter 10

The odd thing was that when Ingrid came into Liz's new house, their house, it all suddenly felt right. The shell, which had been merely walls, became protective, a cocoon. A home. Something neither woman had had for a very long time.

Liz watched Ingrid as her daughter watched something inane on the television. Much watching was going on. She, Ingrid, sat huddled, legs beneath herself, in a lounge chair made large by her beaten compactness. How, Liz wondered, do you put back together a broken human being? Yes, she looks happy enough watching the box in her new pyjamas and dressing gown, but even Ingrid's surface looked fragile.

The rest of us go about in our hard outer layer living our lives in quiet desperation, perhaps quivering a little on a bad day, but fundamentally strong. Ingrid did not appear strong. But she must have been, mustn't she?

Although, come to think of it, the world's people aren't living their lives in quiet desperation anymore. It's loud, still desperate, but loud. Full of anger so old that nobody remembers from where it came and why it won't go away. And now Liz had to strengthen Ingrid's chassis and outer layer, then send her out there, whilst not overly sure why.

"Are you looking forward to the class tomorrow?" she asked her daughter.

Ingrid's head went down immediately; her hands began to flit a bit, agitated. But Liz wanted to feel her out. "I'll stay with you tomorrow, but after that, I'll just drop you there. It's not far from the bus stop. You'll be fine. You've come such a long way."

Ingrid was beginning English classes the next day, to begin to resurrect her language skills. And through this forced interaction with others, some people skills.

"No," Ingrid finally answered.

"It won't be so awful. You'll be ahead of the game; English is your first language. We'll go to a cafe and have a nice lunch afterwards. You can drown your fears in a huge latte."

Because that will help, Liz thought.

"Go to bed now." Ingrid rose and uncurled from the chair.

Shit! "Oh, okay. I'll see you in the morning. Love you."

As it turned out, Ingrid quite enjoyed the class and Liz was able to drop her at the front of the college and went in alone for subsequent lessons, growing more comfortable and confident with each visit. Gradually one fear at a time was being allayed.

One morning Liz dropped Ingrid at the school but didn't have the energy for the dash back home. Financial worries were starting to push forwards as her savings dwindled. So, she bought a cup of coffee and sat, trying not to think, in the park near the Municipal Library. Although the kids on the bright plastic climbing equipment nearby were a little high pitched for comfort, Liz stayed, sitting, sighing. She'd taken to sighing and groaning when rising from a chair. *I'm slipping into early decrepitude,* she thought. *My voice will break soon.*

Liz had always maintained a woman's voice didn't break until she was seventy or eighty and suddenly she would sound like Katherine Hepburn in *On Golden Pond* with a voice like a creaking door slowly closing. Even knowing the movie existed made Liz sigh.

Then her mobile phone rang.

"Mrs Brenner, it's Patricia from the Language College. Can you come? Ros is having some sort of trouble with Ingrid in the classroom."

"What?" Liz asked, even though she'd heard al the words, it was if she couldn't hear meaning.

"She's under a desk... Ros can't get her out..."

"I'll be right there."

Liz ended the call and threw the last of her coffee down, glad that she'd stayed to sit in the park, rather than taking the bus home as she sometimes did.

With a speed she long thought lost, Liz ran and walked and ran to the college, which was only one block from the park.

"In room five," Patricia said as Liz gasped into the office. "Top of the stairs, first on the left."

"Stairs," Liz wheezed, in a split-second of despondency before heading to the carpeted stairs next-door to the office.

Ingrid was huddled under a desk, sitting upright in the womb position, rocking. Liz crawled under, sat down in a similar position, took Ingrid's hand, and the opportunity to regain a normal breathing pattern.

"I'm here," she informed her daughter, following this with deep intakes of breath. "Mum's here."

He was drunk and furious, a volatile mix. The concrete floor was rubbing the skin off where hip and rib bones protruded, with each of his angry rhythmic movements. Face downward, the smell of the always dirty floor violated as much as he did. Permeating, penetrating, so it was hard to become invisible. Can't get away. Chains.

One of the school's computers had been brought into the classroom for a presentation. Being a desktop, it had been fitted with a metal plate and an eyebolt so it could be locked to the wheelable desk or other places via a chain, as a spate of small robberies had left the maintenance team nervous. As the computer was being trundled into the classroom the chain slipped and rattled. The sound dumped Ingrid without warning into a flashback as if from a great height and she landed hard.

"Take this, sweetie. It's just a Xanax."

Mum? Mum?

"I'm here. Just let the tablet melt under your tongue." Liz gently pushed the Xanax into Ingrid's mouth, wishing she could pop one herself. "It's okay; nothing here is going to hurt you."

The mother gently rubbed Ingrid's back with one hand and Ingrid, unusually, let her. With the other hand she used her mobile phone to call Ingrid's new psychiatrist. The call went straight to voice mail, so Liz hung up.

"Could someone call us a taxi?" Liz asked. No one answered but she heard someone leave the room. It was then that she realised Ingrid had wet herself. "Maybe someone could get a towel or two, or paper towels. Something."

Ingrid was slowly making her way back, floating to the surface. She opened her mouth to speak to her mother but was still beyond words. Liz saw her child notice the dampness between her legs and she seemed to shrink further back into herself. The indignities of survival.

* * *

As individual histories bump about it can take some time to decide that life is a game worth playing. Following our first innocent liveliness and a sometimes-abrupt awakening to existence there's a rickety bridge most adolescents struggle to cross. This journey can be made a little easier when beside them friends are taking each step, sharing, laughing, crying together. Perhaps parents are a support in the surrounding structures, letting go but hanging on, tangled in their apron strings and smiling proudly in the right places. It takes time. Some never quite survive. Depression in the young is a killer of light and it's difficult to grow in the dark. Yet others enjoy the trip across and develop cheerfully, moving forward unimpeded toward adulthood.

Ingrid had the standard slow evolution ripped from her psyche and her small body while it was trying to form. Liz found an emergent, damaged woman, her child, needing to be nurtured into growth and healing. In the grey half-light of her awakening Ingrid didn't understand what had happened at the English College. She didn't know why she had ended up beneath a desk. The episode had been sudden and somatic, appearing unrelated to conscious thought. She didn't know what she'd reacted to, or why, just that she had been assailed from within and it had been unpleasant as she fell, saturated with panic. She would not go back to class. Her mother wanted her to, so that fear wouldn't win, but fear always won. Always one with her. She was fear. Ever since Ingrid could remember there was a piece in her chest that was frozen. It ached with fear's cold and when nothing was happening it felt solid. But when the fear hit, there was pain. The frozen dread thawed into a terror that took reality to an edge. One step, no going back.

Nobody really understood. How hard the steps.

"But you need an education, even if it's just enough so you can read again," Liz countered to Ingrid's rejection of her lessons.

"I wet my... myself in front of them."

Ingrid began rocking in the outdoor chair she was sitting in and Liz knew it was time to hold off for a while.

"You were sick," she told Ingrid as an end. "Would you like another orange juice?"

"Can I have what you're having?"

Liz was taken aback, aforth, and in somewhere in between as she examined her near empty wine glass. The weather was too overcast for Liz to feel good about anything, especially the cloudy matter of alcohol for Ingrid. Her daughter was a grown woman, but so new to the world.

"I'm not sure you can have wine with your medications."

"I'll get the pills and stuff. You can read bottles."

Ingrid jumped up and went inside.

"If you went back to school, you could read them yourself," Liz mumbled, and immediately felt contrite. The rain began, softly.

"Shit."

Moving indoors with her wine glass Liz found Ingrid sitting at the dining table, lining up her medications in a tidy row according to size, rocking as she did so.

"What's wrong with me?" she asked her mother, words weighted heavy with self-pity. "I pissed myself in front of my class."

"Aw, sweetie, you're okay. What's really important, is what's right with you. Don't let these medications and a few setbacks fool you. You're all right, a wonderful human being." Ingrid looked doubt filled. "You are very strong," Liz continued. "To survive what you survived…"

"I didn't do anything… All I did was keep breathing. Everybody does that… A fish does that."

"Not everyone would have survived. Not giving up is a strength."

"There was nothing to give up. Don't you see? I was barely alive, that sounds like giving up to me. And now I don't know if I can wake up properly."

"I want to hug you so much. Can I?" Liz asked.

"Okay, but…"

"See? This is a good hug. No one's going to get hurt."

There was a crash and Liz's wine glass lay on the floor, broken and spilling.

"Well, maybe that hurts a little," said Liz, breaking the hug to look sadly at her lost drink.

"I'll get you a new one," Ingrid offered, relieved to be away from touch.

"Mind the glass. I'll clean this up."

"Could you read my medication stuff? I'd like to have a drink with you. Like how you and Anne do."

"Hmm. But just remember alcohol is… for a little bit of fun, not for self-medicating, or drowning your sorrows."

"It's okay Mum, I'll only have one to your every ten."

"Hey! What are you inferring?"

"I don't know what that means. Inferring?"

"Ah, that reminds me, about school… What if I get your class changed, you know, so that the people are different? Would that be okay? A fresh start? Dr Stedman says it's a good idea to go. You trust her, don't you?"

"They treat me funny."

"Who does?"

"The people at school. They're all there because they don't speak English so well, but they have other languages. They can talk to each other. I have no language."

"But you will have. Look how far you've come in a very short while. You're a fast learner."

"What if it happens again? I was scared."

There's a rickety bridge…

"How about we cross that bridge when we come to it?"

11

Chapter 11

"She smells bad, dude. You ought'a do something about it. Almost couldn't fuck her."

"Yeah, well, sometimes I forget she's there. I'll chuck her in the creek when I take the dogs down."

"You should let her have a shower, mate."

"No way. Last time she locked the bloody bathroom door. Had to smash it in. She was trying to get the blade out of me razor by the time I got to her."

"Fuck."

"Haven't had the chain off her since."

"Man. Do you reckon she was gunna use it on you or herself?"

"Don't know. Stupid little cow. She's fucking mental."

"Ingrid? You okay in there? You've been in the shower forever... Ingrid?"

The door was locked. Liz knocked again. To her relief the water turned off.

"You okay?" she called again.

"Yes... I'll be right out."

"You sure you're okay? You sound odd."

"I'm okay."

"All right then. Breakfast's on the table."

"Okay."

Perhaps it's everydayness that helps put people back together. It gently shrouds awareness into a coat of comfortable, which might become not so much happiness but the absence of unhappiness. People can lose themselves in it for years and call it a good life, never quite realising they have, in fact, lost a little of themselves. Even so, maybe it is better to be absorbed in the ordinary than to be always fighting, shadow boxing with the world and living in perpetual crisis. But this snug everydayness can also betray, bringing forth a quietness, a ready ground in which the deferred effects of trauma can unprompted seep. They want to be acknowledged and heard. Need to be heard but take little heed of the readiness or capacity of the listener. They infiltrate sleep to shape malignant, recurring nightmares and twist daydreams into small hells. The casualties of this conflict may find themselves thrashing, drowning in the stream of consciousness, gasping for breath and craving unconsciousness.

"Jam?"

"What?" asked Ingrid entering the kitchen.

"It's not 'what,' it's... Hey, are you all right?"

"Yes."

"You don't look it. You're bleeding! Show me your arm."

"No."

"No, show me. Blood's all up your sleeve."

"No!"

"Ingrid, come on. What happened?"

"I... I don't know. It... "

Ingrid sat down at the table set for breakfast, a little beaten. It's not easy to put in plain words the inexplicable. In the face of the encompassing silence, Liz moved.

"Show me!"

When Liz saw, she was compelled to act.

"I'll 'phone for a taxi," she said.

It took three hours at the hospital. Ingrid sat besieged by the light and noise and rush. Sedation then calm. When the rocking slowed, needles and stitches. Knitting the torn back together. Ingrid was still unable to explain, unable to find a voice and Liz had to call Dr Stedman who hurried to the hospital to stop the doctor treating Ingrid's wound from scheduling her.

"I think she should be admitted," he said. "She's obviously a danger to herself."

"At this stage, there's nothing to be gained by hospitalisation. Ingrid will recover herself at home, in the familiar, with her mum, better than being surrounded by people and sounds she doesn't know. I'll see her daily until this episode has passed," promised Doctor Stedman.

"She cut herself with a razor."

"I know, but it wasn't a suicide attempt. She's been having flashbacks to her trauma. It was more a release."

With this Ingrid was released. Allowed to go. She took home with her a sense of disappointment in herself and a twist of bitterness at the treachery of her psyche.

"Jam?" her mother said.

"What, I mean, I beg your pardon?"

"Jam. Do you want jam on your toast? Breakfast's still ready. But now we'll call it lunch."

"Am I crazy?" asked Ingrid.

"No way. No one could have an ordinary reaction to what you've been through. Don't be hard on yourself. I'll tell you who was crazy, my mother. But don't get me started on that one. No, you're okay. Sane as I am."

"Oh."

"Hey!"

Bread popped up in the toaster, well past being toast, charred to near burnt. Liz swore and scraped the black with a knife. Coffee bubbled on the hotplate, mingling its aromatics with the smoky toast. It bubbled some more then spewed up over the hotplate and the stovetop in a steaming ooze. Liz swore and switched it off. Amongst the debris she and Ingrid spent the next half hour relaxing.

"I'll make breakfast tomorrow," said Ingrid.

"Very wise," said her mother.

12

Chapter 12

Then, without warning, she began to fall, and once the fall had begun the crash was inevitable.

Come on, you. Down to the creek. You stink.

Ingrid didn't mind the creek so much. Sometimes after she'd been dunked he left her there, chained to a tree to dry. From time to time, she was left over night. It could be cold once the sun slipped away, but it meant at least a small peace, a rest from the perpetual shadow of his easily triggered cruelty and gave a short space for stillness. Sometimes too he left Gyro, the German shepherd, with her, after they'd both been bathed, but he would never leave the dog over night. He loved that dog.

She could see the house from her place locked to the tree. Ingrid knew her time of quiet to be over when she saw him leave the compound proper. It was about a ten-minute walk and by the time he reached her, Ingrid was again nearly rigid with a freshly built tension.

He'd be angry.

What are you shaking for? It's not that bloody cold, and don't dawdle, Jon's here. He was your dad's best mate, so be nice to him. Any behaviour like the other day and I'll... Well, let's just say, you'll regret it.

He didn't operate on empty threats. Ingrid knew consequences.

They left her in the dark room after. Bleeding. Her chain wasn't long enough so that she might reach the light switch. She sat on the damp sheeted bed, rocking in her degradation. Between her legs, sore. Burning. Her jaw ached; she felt the nausea of the tired. An overwhelming sense of self-depletion saturated right through to the bone and she sent a request of God, to please let her go. An impulse toward death. He was not in his Heaven and she remained in a half death.

"Mum," she whispered.

And for the first time, "I'm here, sweetie."

"Mum?"

"You're okay. Although it looks like you've ripped your stitches. Let's get you out of bed and cleaned up. See if we need to go to the hospital."

Liz cleaned the wound, found the sutures still intact, so wrestled on to it two band-aids and then wrapped about it a bandage as a safe-guard.

"I think it's okay. How do you feel?" Ingrid, pale and haunted, sat on the closed toilet.

"Why am I such a fucked unit?" she asked.

"You what!? No. No. Oh, hon. No. You are just reacting to a horrible, horrible time. Just because you're out of it, doesn't mean it's out of you... It'll take a bit of time."

"I'm tired, mum."

"I know. I know. But you can still get through. You have a safe place now, to react in."

Liz felt the weariness heavy and wondered how Ingrid could stand it.

"Tomorrow," she said. "Let's go to the beach. Sometimes watching waves is rejuvenating."

"What's rejuvenating?"

"Makes you feel young again."

"Wasn't that crash-hot the first go 'round."

"Well, we'll make sure this your, what is this? Your second childhood. We'll make sure your second childhood has some laughs, and... maybe some chocolate?"

"And ice-cream?"

"Of course."

Ingrid stood, a little less wan, a slight smile and Liz thought the crash cancelled.

Yet the evocative power of the beach brought collision closer. Liz blithely boarded a bus the next morning in a holiday mood, sunglasses sliding down her nose as she fumbled in her enormous tote bag for fare change for the both of them.

"Two adults to Terrigal, please."

They found a seat midway to the back of the bus. Their chat was amiable, nicely shallow, made for easy wading. Nothing deep after the interrupted sleep of the night before. Ingrid, in the window seat watching the world, relatively safe as the bus nudged them toward the beach, was relaxed, smiling.

Liz sat, the huge bag on her lap, easing herself into a benign musing.

"That's a big bag," commented Ingrid.

"Uh huh. I'm ready for anything."

"Even overseas travel?"

"Ah. Sadly, I did leave my passport at home. Remiss."

Congesting traffic slowed the trip. Against the noise of the cars and a group of talkative older women at the front of the bus, Liz and Ingrid lapsed into a forced but comfortable silence. The trip jolted towards three quarters of an hour but finally finished with the smell of salt water and the sound of the cackling nannies moving from the bus towards the bowling club, perhaps to roost in the bingo hall. Liz stood wavering at the bus stop, a little unsure of a direction to take, before deciding to join a surge of pedestrians heading past to her to left. She pulled Ingrid in and they flowed towards the beach.

Fortunately, the beach itself was not crowded. They found a spot and Liz pulled a towel from her bag and Ingrid dragged one from her backpack. They spread them on the warm sand and nestled atop.

"Ingrid, are you all right? You look slightly green."

Jon's here.

Hello, Ingrid. Come over and give your Uncle Jon a kiss... No?

Do as you are fuck-ing told. He. Enunciating each syllable with a malevolent hiss, raised his hand, threatening.

The slap hit so solidly that to call it a slap is inadequate and she was knocked reeling sideways to the floor. They both approached, large with their anger, shrinking her further, but she couldn't disappear altogether. To hide properly it seemed to her, would be to die.

And so, the fall continued.

Ingrid suddenly leant over from where she was seated on her towel and vomited onto the sand. When she was finished she was up and running before Liz could comprehend what was happening. She quickly thrust their towels, sand and all, into her bag. Grabbing it and Ingrid's backpack she headed after her daughter, calling.

"Ingrid, wait!"

Eventually Ingrid dropped. Breathless she sat on the sand, caught somewhere between a scream and a sob. So caught that neither sound could come out, free itself from the tightness of her anguish. Waves of nausea rolled over her as she remembered. Undulating pain.

"Let me die," Ingrid pleaded.

No, he said.

"No," said Liz.

Gently Liz took Ingrid by the hand and raised her to her feet.

He dragged her across the floor, really angry now. I should have left you on that beach.

"No," Ingrid mumbled and pushed Liz away. She began banging her head hard with her own fist as if to make a physical hurt supersede the relived one.

"No," said Liz. "Don't do that."

She tried to grab Ingrid's hands but her child was off again, running frantic.

"Shit!" Liz cried, gathering up the bags again, before chasing after her daughter, sand fountaining from her feet over nearby beachgoers.

"Hey!" yelled one of them. "Watch what you're doing."

He slapped her again. This time blessed unconsciousness. But when she awoke with the taste of blood salting her awareness, they were taking her, from the back and the front. She tried desperately to dissociate from the pain and succeeded in some way but the smell of their odour kept forcing her present and she heard herself whimpering like a hurt animal. 'She's coming,' he said, and irate she spat in his face before everything erupted in red.

"Ingrid?"

Liz could tell by Ingrid's eyes that she was distant, away, tormented in a bad place. She was still thumping at her own head with her balled hand; her nose bloodied.

"Please stop that," Liz begged. "I won't touch you, but please stop."

Ingrid gave no indication of having heard. At a loss, Liz pulled out her mobile phone and searched through the name index for Doctor Stedman's number. She connected with the receptionist and blurted out her concern in a disjointed and anxious jumble of words. Soon the doctor was on the line and Liz repeated her dilemma with a slightly more coherence. Doctor Stedman said she would come straight to them.

Time brought both mother and daughter forward and Liz managed to seat Ingrid on a towel before dropping down beside her, carefully, to avoid touch. Afraid. Ready for anything, she murmured at herself. Acutely feeling this, a new sense of inadequacy, jab defiant, mocking her buoyancy of the earlier bus ride. Ingrid rocked, still occasionally hitting at herself in a rhythmic anger.

"Listen to the surf," Liz suggested. "Hear it? No. Please don't hit yourself. Listen. That's what forever sounds like. Not what's in your head. You'll see. The past will fade away a little and it won't always hurt so much."

Liz hoped she was telling the truth. Ingrid still rocked, far away. Deep, within herself. Then she hit out again. The surf roared. More blood oozed from Ingrid's nose and it began to leave a trail down her blouse. Grabbing her tote bag and digging into it, Liz rummaged out some tissues but then held them, ineffectual.

"Please don't," she begged, as Ingrid hit herself again.

"Liz." Doctor Stedman stood over them, holding her high heel shoes in her left hand. She moved to kneel in front of Ingrid. "There's blood." As if to illustrate how it came to be, Ingrid hit herself again, a solid right. "How long as she been like this?"

"Nearly an hour, I think." Liz answered, looking at her watch to find herself so immersed in maternal concern that she was unable to focus on the numbers, let alone see the hands of time.

"I'm sorry, but I think she'll have to go to hospital."

Liz nodded, just wanting her child safe. Ingrid smacked herself again.

"Let's get her to the road," said the doctor. "And I'll run and get my car."

They managed to raise Ingrid to her feet. Liz grabbed the bags and towel in one hand and held fast to Ingrid's wrist with the other, afraid that she might run again. Ingrid fought but Liz held grim, cursing silently her cumbersome tote bag.

Come here, bitch. He grabbed her and not waiting for her to gain her feet, pulled her towards the dark cupboard. She tripped further on the chain around her leg and he quickly had her unlocked and free of it.

The doctor took Ingrid's other arm and they led her with difficulty from the beach. Bemused onlookers turned their heads and watched their struggling progress without offering comment or assistance. By the time they reached kerbside Ingrid had shrunk subdued into herself further. Drenched in an old powerlessness that held her as tightly as Liz, she relinquished her struggle. Her mother gripping her arm with a diligence born of trepidation and the nearness of noisy, hurried cars, noticed the surrender but held on afraid. There was a small relief when the doctor's car pulled along side and they were able to slide into the back seat. He threw her hard into the cupboard and shut her in the darkness. Ingrid cowered against the door, flinching as Liz secured the seatbelt for her and checked that the door was locked.

She counted. She counted to fend off the fear that ate at her insides and shook her exterior like the cold. Then she began to lose her numbers, fade a bit and repeat some. Counted to fifty but stumbled confused and found herself back at number thirty-five. She began again from one, as punishment. Start again. Start again. Her back hurt. There was no room to straighten. She needed to pee. Twenty, what? Twenty-five, six? She couldn't remember. One, two, three. Then she couldn't recollect her birth date. The numbers were gone. Time had left her with nothing. The day, the month, the year, all were lost. The dark was unbearable. She fell into panic, scratched at the walls again, trying to find light. Scratched, frantic and she wet herself. One, two, three... For a time fell asleep sucking her bloodied fingers and when she awoke smothered still by the dark, she fell again into a great panic.

Scheduling Ingrid into the psychiatric ward was expedited with, unusually, barely a wait in Accident and Emergency. Liz sat swamped in guilt for having her child again placed in the ward, but she knew Ingrid's behaviour was out of her sphere of experience for the moment, beyond the panacea of a mother's love. Ingrid still pounded her head until the sedation took affect, bruising beginning to show on her face, cheek, and around her right eye. She lay awake but lost on the hospital bed, neither acknowledging Liz nor any of the medical staff, until finally she slept.

After mislaid days in the ward Ingrid became aware and was immediately flattened, trampled by the comprehension of where she was, once more confined and medicated. This crash landing in the ward depleted further her weakened spirit; her fragile optimism imprisoned now in a close fitting, suffocating dark and she was alone, precariously on the edge of the past and the present. She began to count, one, two, three. Starting over.

13

Chapter 13

Exhausted to the marrow, Liz drooped with a weak 'flump' onto the lounge, dropping bags without care at her feet. She sat for a long time empty. Then it began to build, a burgundy mix of anger and sadness. Red and blue, infiltrating her consciousness to fog over and near corrode her heart. She could feel it beat unsteady, now anger, now gloom, now anger, now gloom. Fast then slow.

"Fuck. Fuck. Fuck!"

The anger was two-sided, razorblade sharp. One side, anger at herself for her own perceived inadequacy; Ingrid needing help, Liz running around feeble with a giant tote bag. Anger too, at the actual, so easily tangible, relief she felt now that her daughter was protected and safe in the hospital. Able to relax at night knowing she would not wake to find Ingrid, and blood. Someone else had responsibility and Liz was relieved. She felt betrayed by this sense of respite, as if Ingrid were a burden to be passed.

Now gloom. She, great with anticipation, had brought a daughter into the world, watched as her child grew, learned, laughed, and then, she, a mother, had lost her. Did not hold her hand. Turned her back for those few life altering seconds. Let down her guard, lost her child. Years, hard years, and now the return, another chance, but she couldn't put her daughter back together again. She had let Ingrid down once more.

Evening shade darkened the room and Liz huddled into her dejection. She needed light but she couldn't raise herself from the lounge to switch on the overhead lamps. She wept a little.

***

"What's Ingrid Brenner doing?"

"She appears to be counting. Rocking and counting."

The nurses looked at each and shrugged. They'd pretty much seen it all. Rocking and counting was tame. Self-soothing behaviours were not uncommon.

"She hasn't eaten since yesterday."

"Yeah, I know. There are some sandwiches left over from dinner, do you want to try her?"

"Sure."

"Don't touch her though, she's hyper-sensitive to touch."

"Okay. Five dollars says I can get her to eat a sandwich."

"You're on."

***

Inertia, growing too tired to feel, brought Liz back from her guilt trip, her baggage returned to the overhead compartment of her subconscious, to wait for the next journey out. She felt vaguely hungry, distinctly thirsty. For a nice glass of chilled Chablis. If only she could move.

***

"How'd you go with Ingrid and the sandwich?"

"I owe you five dollars."

The door opened and the craved for light hit painfully the eyes. She was dragged from the cupboard and as she lay on the floor felt the cold of the manacle wrapped around her ankle.

'Here, eat this.'

A leg of greasy dripping chicken was thrust in her face and immediately she recoiled, nauseous, gagging.

'Eat it, you stupid cow. You've been in the cupboard for four days; do you want to die?'

'Water,' she said.

'You ungrateful little bitch! Down the creek, come on! I'll give you fucking water!'

"Looks like Ingrid needs some medication. What's she written up for?"

* * *

A glass of Chardonnay from a box was the best Liz could do. The cask was nearly empty so she pulled the wine bladder from the cardboard container and snipped off its corner with the kitchen scissors, to pour a full glass from the cut. Liz eased back into the lounge.

The telephone infiltrated then dragged Liz from an instantly forgotten dream. She flew from the couch to the 'phone table before she was quite awake and aware.

"Is that Elizabeth Brenner?"

"What? Yes. Who?"

"Good morning, it's Joan from Doctor Stedman's office. Your mobile seems to be off."

"Morning? What? Oh, okay. I'm awake now. What can I do for you? Is Ingrid all right?"

"We haven't talked to the hospital yet, today. The Doctor was wondering if you could possibly come in and see her this morning at eleven? She has a cancellation and has some things she'd like to discuss with you."

"Things? Eleven? Um, yes, that's fine."

"Okay, we'll see you then. Bye, bye."

"Bye."

Telephone back in its cradle, Liz stood for a while on one spot swaying with indecision.

'Shower before food,' she determined, nudging away a keen self-impatience. Still, she wore yesterday's clothes and felt the taint of yesterday's mood. "New day," she said, shaking them off.

A pelting hot shower, short and sweet, left Liz with a sense that she might withstand another day yet. Heavy-duty espresso strengthened further this still susceptible sense of survival. Fortified, she felt ready to battle the malevolent toaster, and on conquering this would meet with Doctor Stedman and then face the hospital again.

The smoke alert screamed from the ceiling that the toast was ready and Liz's calm decomposed, shattering in the shrill. She jabbed at the alarm with a broom handle and in the following quiet exploded a few expletives.

"You bastard toaster! You're on the lowest bloody setting! Why do you keep doing this? Jeez."

Exasperated, Liz scraped the charred vestige of her toast and spread jam on what remained.

An hour on, from the bus stop as she waited, Liz could see the sun ricocheting off the Brisbane Water blue and in the colour the world seemed a little bit kinder. She found a small peace. Amidst the raucousness of the morning noise, traffic snarling, birds squawking without music, Liz remembered to breathe and felt her mind still, if just for a moment, before she counted out bus change from her purse and slipped back into the harshness of movement.

The bus appeared loaded with small unquiet bouncing children. Amidst the colourful noise Liz found a seat next to a young person, whose headphones hissed out a sound as mellifluous as a jackhammer. She was uncalmed, on the verge of a headline; 'woman goes berserk on local bus - jams young person's phone up...'

Steady. Too much coffee.

The bus ride was mercifully quick and Liz spilled onto the pavement with the last of the passengers at Gosford Station. There was a half hour until her appointment with Doctor Stedman. After a second's hesitation and against all self-advice, Liz went for a cappuccino, to reflect on the possible 'things' the doctor might wish to discuss. But basically, she sat staring into space, losing herself and Ingrid momentarily to the refuge of nothingness.

By the time she did reach the doctor's office, Liz was experiencing caffeine induced heart palpitations and once seated her hands were shaking the copy of the *Reader's Digest* she'd picked up to skim.

"The Doctor won't be long. Would you like a coffee while you wait?" the receptionist asked.

"No, thank you. I've got quite a coffee buzz going on all ready. That, or I'm having a coronary."

"Well, let me know if you need CPR, or change your mind about a coffee."

"Thank you, I will."

Liz smiled a shaky smile and opened the *Digest* and found a story of a man who'd sawn off his own leg with a penknife to free himself, after three days under a bone-crushing fallen rock. Then, he hopped four miles to a road to flag down a passing motorist with his blood-soaked bandanna, only to be involved in a car accident on the way to the hospital.

"Mrs. Brenner? Come in." When she looked up from the *Digest* the doctor waved Liz through to her office. "Have a seat." Liz avoided the couch and sat in a comfy chair with a sudden straight-backed tension. "I saw Ingrid earlier," Doctor Stedman added. "She seems more aware today."

"Oh, that's good. Can she come home?"

"Not quite yet, but she's been moved to the open ward."

"Great. She'll like that better."

"She's not eating."

"Oh. Is it the food? I could bring her in something cooked at home."

The doctor smirked. "I know the food in there isn't very appetising, but I think the food itself isn't the issue."

"Well, my cooking's hardly gourmet either," said Liz, thinking of her charred breakfast toast.

"It may be directly related to what she remembered. The flashback."

"What did she remember?"

"Well, not that I could tell you without Ingrid's expressed permission, but she hasn't talked yet. It obviously made her very distraught and sent her back into an old pattern of behaviour. Old coping mechanisms."

"But you think she'll find her way back out of it?"

"She's a fighter." The doctor smiled. "What I really wanted to talk about, was you."

"Me? There's nothing much to talk about there."

The doctor smiled again. "I think there is."

"I might be a bit screwy but I don't think I need analysis or anything."

"No, I'm not implying that you do. But it's occurred to me that you might benefit from a bit of counselling. Given that you lived years not knowing if your child was alive or dead."

"I guess."

"... And then, when you do get her back, and she is so traumatised, you've literally become a carer for someone you don't really know. It can't be how you dreamed of the homecoming."

"I gave up on happy endings a long time ago. Not that this is unhappy..."

"Do you allow yourself to feel a of bit resentment? A little anger at the circumstances?"

"Yes, I suppose so."

"Or do you believe you have no right to feel such things? My guess is, you're probably giving yourself a hard time."

"I should be grateful. I've got my daughter back."

"But you haven't, have you? This is not the same person that was taken from you."

"I know. But she's still..."

"Ingrid's not the only hurt party. I think that some counselling will help you and perhaps as Ingrid recovers some more, you can go together."

"But..."

"Think about it. It can only help Ingrid if you've resolved some of the ambiguous feelings that this sort of trauma can bring to the surface."

"I'm not traumatised. Ingrid's the one..."

"Aren't you? The woman I found on the beach certainly looked distressed to me."

"It was just a trick of the light," Liz said, smiling.

"Okay. Anyway, here's a number of a colleague. I'd like it if you arranged a visit with her. She's very good."

"You can't see me?"

"It's better for Ingrid if she feels I'm not divided in my loyalties."

"Okay. You mean so she can have a whinge about me if she feels the need?"

"Something like that. Now, the other thing I wanted to speak to you about is Ingrid's speech difficulties. Perhaps she might benefit from some intensive speech therapy."

"But I thought it was just a matter of time with that."

"Well, yes and no. You must remember, as far as we know Ingrid has never had a conversation with anyone. Her language is confused and uncertain."

"She's getting a little better."

"But there is no easy flow. You see, the brain has a type of language centre and it's thought if a child doesn't acquire the fundamentals of grammar and speech by the age of twelve or so, it becomes very difficult to learn. The language Ingrid did have when she was kidnapped disappeared with the lack of use and I guess it was replaced with a mixture of thought shorthand and some words she did remember. Language was completely internalised and didn't utilise the spoken word at all."

"Don't you think she'll get back what she had?"

"It's hard to say. A lot of adults have trouble learning a second language, whereas children can just pick it up. Ingrid might always have some difficulty with syntax and language complexities but speech therapy could help her past the anxieties and hesitancy she has and teach her some shortcuts that will make speech a little easier. It's good that you started her at the language school, and speech therapy will reinforce what she's learning there too."

"I want to do whatever I can to help."

"Well, ringing that number I gave you is a start." The doctor stood up, smiling. "Remember, you have to look after you too."

"I'll give it some thought."

* * *

There was still four hours until the hospital's afternoon visiting time. Liz went for a coffee and some lunch, a long lunch, and another coffee, followed by a bit of caffeined-up jittery shopping.

"I bought a new toaster," she told Ingrid when she was finally permitted entry onto the ward.

14

Chapter 14

Dreary skies, grey ideas over her morning coffee, before Liz pushed away the elementally related funk and headed for the bus stop. The sun seeped out but the weather had an icy demeanour, promising a cold autumn and Liz shook a little in her shoes. She was sad that Ingrid had missed most of the summer hermetically sealed into the air-conditioned climate of the hospital ward, seasonally devoid.

It was not visiting hours, but Liz was allowed entry to help Ingrid gather her gear for going home. Happy to be leaving, Ingrid was pacing about buoyant in barely controlled impatience.

"Okay," said Liz. "Is that everything?"

"Yes, yes, yes."

"Are you eager to be out of here?"

"Yes, yes, yes."

"Then, let's go."

Things, as might be expected, moved slowly then. They weren't to leave until medications were sent from the pharmacy and certain papers had been pushed. Disappointed at the sluggish pace of hospital protocol, Ingrid sat in the lounge-room containing herself not quite with a rhythmic tapping of her right foot.

"Shall we have a coffee?" Liz asked.

It was decaffeinated but making the drinks gave Ingrid a task to stave off her pervasive impatience for a few more minutes. It was an hour of delay, minutes that for Ingrid slowly ticked over liked defective gearing.

Finally they were allowed through the last of the electronic doors to the cool autumn freedom. Ingrid sighed deeply.

"The air is different feeling out here. Free."

"Do you want to go home or go for real coffee?"

Ingrid was torn. "Both."

"Let's get a taxi and get home and have a coffee."

"But we don't have fluff." Ingrid pointed out, meaning the froth atop a cappuccino.

"Yes, we are fluff-less. How quickly do you want to get home?"

"I am free. Let's have a shop coffee first, can we?"

Liz smiled. "We can. And if we time it right, there'll be a bus when we're done."

Of course, they just missed a bus, but Ingrid sat happily while they waited for the next one.

"School tomorrow?"

"No. Two things, tomorrow is Saturday and it's semester break."

"Oh. Holidays. How long?"

"Another week. But they want you to do the year over, because you missed so much."

"Again, again?"

It would be Ingrid's third time starting the course from the beginning.

"Think how far ahead of the others you'll be."

"Yeah. Am I so stupid?"

"No, you aren't stupid! You've a lot to catch up on, is all. After you've learnt to read, there's the next step. Learning maths, and science, or music, or, well, lots of stuff. It'll be exciting."

"Is maths exciting?"

"Not for me. But some people are strangely stimulated by it. You draw well; you might find art is your subject."

"What's art?"

"Um, the science of colouring in."

"And staying in the lines?"

"Not necessarily. I was just being a bit glib. Art is a big subject. I'll show you more on the Internet dot COM, when we get home if you like. It's hard to explain art without examples."

"Okay. Why'd you say, 'dot com'?"

"I don't know, just being silly. Is this our bus? What number's that?"

Ingrid was through the front door of their home before Liz could remove the key from the lock.

"My bed," she called from her room in happy reunion. "My stuff."

A childlike easy glee settled over the house and Liz nestled into it as a soft, warm cushion. It called for a fragrant domesticity and she began to defrost in the microwave a joint of lamb for roasting.

"Can I help?" Ingrid asked, entering the kitchen.

"You want to peel some potatoes?"

"How?"

"I'll show you."

Ingrid was thorough in execution and wielded the peeler with the intent of someone new to a job. She impressed the boss.

"Hey, that's great. Not a hint of peel left. Here, you can do these carrots too. And these parsnips."

"Boy, we eat lots of stuff out of dirt."

"Had enough of peeling?"

"No. It's okay. I like to help."

"How about I put some of my olden day's music on? It makes chores easier."

"Fleetwood Mac?"

"You remember?" Liz asked remembering herself how they used to play disks up loud on heavy housework days. Seeing Ingrid bopping around the flat with a feather duster while Liz asphyxiated herself with a spray cleaner. Happy days.

"Yes. Barney."

"That's right! Barney, the vacuum cleaner, may he rest in pieces. How loud he was."

"Louder than Pink Floyd."

"Or Meatloaf. I think we should go with a food theme now. I'll put on The Cranberries."

Liz stood in front of the sound system for a minute happily, her heart melting over the first reminiscence shared with Ingrid since her return.

15

Chapter 15

Her awakening the next morning was untroubled, soft, of a sort Ingrid hadn't experienced often. Gentle, still slightly tinctured in sleep, she stretched each limb in the way of those that felt safe. She could smell coffee brewing and her mother scuffing about in her slippers on the tiled kitchen floor.

"Good morning!" Ingrid called to her mother.

"Coffee?" was the answer.

"Yes, please."

Luxuries, like morning hot drink deliveries to bedside, were still new enough in Ingrid's life to make her dichotomously happy and uncomfortable at the same time.

Her mother came into her room carrying two mugs. "Mind if I join you?" she asked, placing the coffees on the bedside table.

"No."

Ingrid moved over some, patting the bed in welcome, to let her mother join her there.

"Well," Liz began. "I think we should start the day off slow. Leisurely breakfast in our PJs, then dress, walk, amble even, down to the shops for some snacks and a sloth-filled afternoon in front of the telly with chocolate and other things that might put some weight on you."

That same dichotomous twinge hurt Ingrid again. She smiled at her mother and nodded in happy agreement but felt a little swamped. Probably not swamped so much as up to her ankles, still able to get away, but there was discomfort and Ingrid couldn't read her own feelings well enough to sort them. Her mother seemed to have an inkling.

"I'll leave you with your coffee and go defrost some bacon for brekkie. We need more lard in our lives," she said making an intuitive retreat.

Alone, Ingrid vented her frustration, she hit at herself, but only once, to the side of her head. Her old mother and her new mother were the best things that had happened in her life ever, yet she felt this discomfort. Ingrid wanted to be free to love her mother without restriction or constriction, but the past kept seeping without permission through her like a repetitive infection. She hit out again.

"Everything all right in there?" her mother called from the kitchen, a small note of concern pitching her voice higher.

"Yes. It's okay," Ingrid returned, mollifying. She decided to use movement as a distraction and slipped out of her bed, made it, and walked her now tepid coffee into the kitchen.

"You should have your dressing gown on," Liz nagged maternally.

"Yes," said Ingrid, but sat down at the kitchen table. "We will have laughing movies?" she asked.

"Comedies? Yes, of course. That and with the chocolate, we're going to laugh ourselves sick."

Ingrid looked worried.

"That's just an expression. Perhaps we will just laugh enough that our drink splurts out of our nose?"

Ingrid still wasn't looking happy.

"Don't knock it till you've tried it. If you're laughing that much," her mother explained. "...that what you're drinking at the time splurts out of your nose, you're having a good time."

"You're weird."

"Yes, so you've said. I know, sweetheart... Anyhow, how about you oversee the toast?"

"New toaster."

"Uh huh. Look, still so clean, you could do rocket surgery in there," Liz said, proudly.

"What?"

"Nothing. You want some cooked tomato with your bacon and eggs?"

"No, thank you. Should I put our fork and knives out first?" Ingrid asked, waving her arm over the unlaid table.

"If you like. But say it the other way around. Knife and fork."

"What? Why?"

"I don't know, it sounds kind of rude that way 'round if you say it quickly. Fork 'n' knife."

Ingrid smiled a little on hearing it, and an ounce or more of her earlier discomfort bleed away. She moved to the fork and knife drawer to begin laying the table for the morning meal. Her mother hummed undaunted over the frying pan as the smoke alarm began to chirp and breakfast became somewhat loud but not mentally uncomfortable for Ingrid. Liz poked the now screaming alarm with the broom handle, mumbling at the irony of 'life saving whatnots that scare a person to death,' while an egg, which had been waiting patiently on the bench to be cracked open into the fry-pan, began to roll in that mythical lemming-like way towards the edge of the kitchen counter. No one was hurt in the scramble.

Breakfast safely over, Ingrid, morning medicated, dressed and met her mother at the front door, ready for their amble to the video store.

"Change that to a brisk walk," said Liz. "It's quite chilly out here."

"Chilli?" asked Ingrid, wondering whether her mother used some words in the wrong places. As far as she had learned, chilli was food.

"Cold," said Liz.

"But that time we ate it, it was hot."

"Sorry, what?"

"The chilli," Ingrid tried to explain, as they reached the front gate and her mother checked the letterbox. "We ate it, it was hot."

"Oh, I got you. The chilli that you eat is spelt, cee, aitch, eye, ell, ell, eye. And the chilly that is cold is cee, aitch, eye, ell, ell, why. It can all get a bit confusing." Liz threw the junk mail straight into the recycle bin. "Even I have trouble with English," she said, as they headed out on to the footpath and towards the local shops.

Ingrid doubted. She'd never seen her mother in trouble. Not like Ingrid knew trouble.

There was an interlude, an encouraging lull, where Ingrid was able to halt thinking for a quiet minute as they walked, marching themselves into an easy rhythm.

The main street greeted them aggressively, restoring some of Ingrid's earlier fretfulness, with its loud busyness. Cars, people, many of them, hurrying towards something, were a shock to her fragile senses. Movement, noise, smells, all a tad overwhelming, so that they appeared exaggerated to her. Ingrid stopped abruptly and put her index fingers in her ears. She could see her mother was a bit surprised by the action.

"Oh, sorry. Saturdays. I should have thought. Come on, let's get to the chemist quickly, I'll get you some industrial strength earplugs."

Once the soft pink plugs were fitted into her ears Ingrid felt a little better. Movement was still 'loud' but she felt she could cope if she closed her eyes for a second. She wanted to hold her mother's hand for comfort but also didn't want to. Conflict always.

Liz chose an arm full of different lollies, 'in case some of them were ick,' she said. Ingrid wandered the aisles wishing her reading had improved more. Finally, back in the snack section with her mother, she picked up a box of chips because she liked the picture on the cover.

"Okay," said Liz taking it from her. "Let's get these and the munchies and get out of here."

They added fruit and nut chocolate and her mother had Ingrid off the main road, onto the back streets in no time. Soon they slipped into their compatible stride beside each other. Ingrid, carrying the food supplies, un-muted her ears with her spare hand and slid the new ear plugs into her jeans' pocket.

At the corner house of their street, the dog that lived there ran up to it's front fence to say hello making them both jump.

"Hi," returned Liz, quickly over the shock. "What's your name?" She reached over the fence and fumbled around the collar until she came to the dog tag. "Hmm. Let's see, hello... 'micro-chipped'. Well, that can't be right..."

Ingrid also put her hand over the fence to pat the friendly dog, his tail wagging madly at the attention. This precipitated an unexpected memory of 'Gyro' who had been beside her back at the farm, and Ingrid felt herself go a little unsteady. *Both she and Gyro down by the creek, chained to the tree, waiting. He for his dinner, she for, God knows what.*

"Hey, are you okay?" Ingrid heard her mother ask.

Ingrid nodded an affirmative, trying so very hard to stay in the present.

"Do you need a tablet?" Liz asked, delving into her handbag.

Ingrid nodded again. Her mother already had the bottle opened and handed over a Xanax.

"Take deep breaths, hon," she said, soothingly.

There was a time when Ingrid would have sat down where she was, hugging her own legs to herself, unmovable, until she felt better. Medications and her mother explaining that, 'some behaviours were for home only,' had moved this away from being an immediate impulse, but it was there now and she had to fight it.

"Home," she finally managed.

"You bet," said Liz, picking up the bags, adding a farewell to the dog. "Goodbye, Mr Chips."

"Did they find a dog when they found me?" Ingrid asked.

"What? No. I don't know. I could find out for you on Monday?"

"Okay."

Movies, chocolate, crisps and home delivered pizza, later made Ingrid feel sick. But a happy sick.

16

Chapter 16

Liz had not heard back from the Major Crime Squad as to Gyro's fate. Ingrid thought perhaps he was dead and almost let herself feel sad over his loss but pulled away from the feeling at the last second, intimidated by the alien-ness of the emotion. Her mother left a message with the Police a second time, but by Wednesday they still had no answer.

"Was he a nice dog?" Liz asked.

"My friend," Ingrid answered. "Bigger than Mr Chips. A shepherd."

"Oo, they can be nasty."

"He was."

"But not with you?"

"He came as a puppy. We played. I'll have a shower now."

Ingrid rose quickly and headed for her bedroom, unsure how to deal with an onslaught of serrated near memories that were again trying to snag on, and open, old wounds.

"Closed, stay closed," she begged them. "Fuck," came out a whisper, so her mother couldn't hear. "I'm not ready."

Ingrid grabbed her morning medications and threw them down her neck, swallowing without water. Gulped sedation too, feeling the memories cracking open, tearing and stuff rising to her consciousness like lava, burning as it flared upward. When she arrived in the bathroom, arms full of fresh clothes, Ingrid tossed them on the closed loo and gently shut and locked the bathroom door on her mother.

There was a disposable razor in the shower and Ingrid levered open the plastic shell with a pair of eyebrow tweezers and carefully took out the blades. The shower water had warmed, and naked, she sank to the floor with the blades, ready. It was not a conscious thought, but maybe a subliminal plea that a part of her might bleed out the memories, let out the pain, before they reached her proper, a red, silent scream.

"Fuck," she whispered again, knowing this was not an 'adult' way to deal with turmoil, but the compulsion to cut felt stronger than she did.

"Come on retard, I haven't got all day."

Jon pushed her backward towards the wall and she tripped over her own chain, as clumsily as he walked with his jeans around his ankles. He pulled down her underwear and thrust in with one harsh movement. Within seconds she could feel blood running down her leg from the tear.

"Fuck!" Jon yelled, pulling away abruptly.

He, her captor, rushed into the room, ready to strike her, yelling, "What did she do?"

"Nothing. Your fucking dog tried to take a piece out of my leg!" Jon uttered, pulling up his jeans.

"Yeah, I've been training him to catch vermin. Good boy, Gyro."

"Well, ha. That son of a bitch, you ought 'a watch him. Fuck... I need a beer. Got any antiseptic? He bloody punctured me."

The shower water was still warm, although some time had passed. Ingrid was surprised not to see blood running anywhere although she could feel it on her thighs. But the blades were clean, unused. Much relieved, but still shaky, she left the shower stall and while dripping water onto the bathroom floor, gently wrapped the blades in tissues, plus a dry face washer, to stash them carefully at the back of the vanity unit. She didn't know why.

Dry and dressed, Ingrid searched out her mother. She found Liz sitting on the lounge, legs folded beneath herself.

"I've been thinking," Liz began as Ingrid entered the room, and Ingrid had to smile at the normalcy. "We should open you a bank account, but I'm not sure where to begin with the identification you'll need. I think I have your Birth Certificate somewhere..."

"What for? Bank account?"

"For you to put your money in."

"I don't have money."

"I've been thinking about that, too." Ingrid smiled again and sat down on the lounge to hear her mother out. "One," continue Liz. "You're probably entitled to victim's compensation and, two; you can also apply for a disability pension."

"What's that?"

"Well, compensation is like replacing everything you lost, and a pension is a payment the government give you every fortnight if you can't work."

"Replace, like Gyro? We replace Gyro?"

"Well, yes and no, it's more about things, the life, you could have had if you hadn't been kidnapped."

"How do we know what I could have had?" Ingrid asked, an ability to speculate yet untried.

"We don't, but you lost a lot of years that we can never replace, but we can make your future a little easier."

"So, we can get a dog?"

Liz looked at Ingrid and smiled, a little sadly, at her innocent understanding of recompense. "Hmm, maybe. But first things first. My savings are dwindling and we need to live on something."

"What are savings?" Ingrid asked but then saw that her mother looked tired. "I will make you a coffee."

Ingrid was into the kitchen instantly, the kettle switched on and cups made ready. In the stillness, waiting, she felt some residue of the earlier remembering but pushed it aside. The thought of the blades, secreted in the bathroom cabinet, somehow now comforting. An outlet, if things became far too much to endure. An imperfect alternative, but Ingrid's own choice. A choosing he had denied her. There was so much inside. It, without question, needed to be let out.

"Biscuit?" she called, like her mother would, positions reversed, bringing herself back to now.

"No thanks, hon."

Ingrid moved back into the lounge room, carefully holding the coffees ahead of herself, avoiding spillage. Her mother had not moved, stuck in a thoughtful place.

"Thanks, hon."

"Will the card from school help? It has photo."

"Yes, your student card, that'll be good. I'll go on the net and see how many points you need for a bank account. I think it's a hundred."

Ingrid wanted to know what game the bank played that she needed to score a hundred, but thought her mother did not want questions today, just answers.

"We'll go into town after lunch and get the forms from Social or Centrelink, whatever it's called now," said Liz, sounding resolute.

Ingrid asked, "Will there be crowds?" She wasn't feeling particularly social.

"I think there's always a queue. But we'll have ourselves a treat afterwards, as reward. Maybe something with cream..."

"So," began Ingrid, trying to get it straight. "We're getting forms for a?"

"Pension."

"Because I can't work yet?"

"That's right, a Disability Pension."

"Dis... disability?"

"That's when a condition prevents you from doing something, like visually impaired, or hearing impaired."

"Like not drive a car on a road if you're blind?"

"That's right."

"Not blind or deaf. I am disabled?"

"You have a problem that prevents you from working at the moment," Liz explained.

Ingrid thought of her emotional disturbance in the shower not more than an hour before.

"I am feeling impaired," she said.

17

Chapter 17

There was rain. Not drought ending, but sufficient to create road holes full of chaos and flash flooding. Ingrid stood blue at the back glass doors, watching, a little resentful, confined. She had no reason to be outdoors but was maddened by the detainment inside. This feeling, entwined with the easily awoken mass of panic with which her past had endowed, elbowed any sense of cosiness well out of the way. 'Cabin fever' her mother called it, as Ingrid paced to the doors and away, rhythmic walking inciting more edginess.

"What about a jigsaw puzzle?" Liz suggested, giving up trying to read, with Ingrid striding in and out of her peripheral vision. "I know you don't like to feel confined, but this won't last forever."

"It has."

"Well, should we go out early anyway? Bugger the rain. Pleurisy is something I've never tried before."

"Pleurisy?"

"Nothing. Although an umbrella will be useless against that wind. No, hold up, there's the 'phone. Do you want to try and answer it?"

Ingrid nodded vigorously negative; she had not mastered language enough to survive tele-marketers.

"Hello?" said Liz into the handpiece. "Robert! Well, it's been a long time! Is this about Gyro? The dog? Sorry? Jon Ingram, yes. He was one of my husband's drinking buddies. Haven't seen him for decades."

Ingrid had paled and slipped unsteady to the lounge.

"Arrested?" Liz looked at Ingrid and saw anguish. "Um Robert, was he a part of what happened to... Sorry? Did he actually admit to doing anything to Ingrid? She's... What? Christ! But he thinks she's dead? Small mercy... Look I think I have to go. Ingrid's... Yes. Okay. She has an appointment with her doctor at two, I could meet you then. Where? Okay, see you this arvo. Bye."

Mother moved to daughter and they sat sharing a disturbed silence for a while. Shocked, hurt into a deeper unquiet, Ingrid shook. Liz gently placed her hand on her child's knee.

"I am with you," she said softly.

* * *

"I can see you're upset," said Dr Stedman. "Your mother told me the police have arrested Jon Ingram. When did you meet him?"

Ingrid was rocking within a comfortable chair, struggling against an oversupply of sensation. She knew not how to be still.

"I don't remember. I want to forget," she told the psychiatrist. There were razor blades in the bathroom cabinet. She could feel the pull. Tight around her ankle. Pain kept her awake at night. The manacle. *Get this fucking off me!* she had wanted to scream but had lost her voice a long, long time before.

"Stay with me, Ingrid."

The doctor's voice, far and near. Ingrid not alive, nor dead.

"He will kill me," she said.

"Who? Jon Ingram?"

No. No.

"Here's your Uncle Jon. Now play nice. He wants to go hunting with me after, and you don't want to be the rabbit, do you? Eh? Do you?"

No. No.

"Ingrid? Ingrid, it's not happening now. Jon Ingram is in gaol. That was the past. Come forward to me. You are safe, here, in my office."

He is here. In me. Always in me. Jon goes away. He is here. Now. In me.

"Ingrid? Ingrid, what is his name?"

"No."

Under the bed. Safe. No, he pulls the chain hard.

"Come here, bitch. Why do you fucking struggle? You know you can't win. Jon's waiting."

Under the bed. Safe. The pain, ankle, shackle digs in skin. Want to scream. But no noise. Hang on.

"Leave her. There's blood coming from under there."

"No, fuck her!"

"Ingrid?"

The pain in her ankle was extreme.

"Ingrid?" the doctor called softly. "Tell me what's happening."

"No. It's bad."

"It's okay. You can tell me."

"No."

"It's okay, Ingrid."

"He dragged me on the concrete."

"Was Ingram there?"

It's dark.

"Yes," Ingrid said.

"Okay. Are you all right? You've done well today. Ingrid, are you back?"

Neither dead, nor alive.

"Ingrid?"

"Yes?"

"You're back? I know this is hard for you. You're safe now. Can you feel the chair you're in?"

"Don't want to feel any more."

"No, that's understandable. Remember, this helps you to ground yourself. Feel the chair, the fabric. That's it. Feel the floor under your feet."

"My ankle's sore."

"You can rub it."

"They were wrong, weren't they?"

"Who?"

"No. They were bad."

"Who? The men who kidnapped you? They were bad. Evil."

"Evil," Ingrid mimicked, trying out the word. "Yes."

"Now, all the memories can go away until Thursday and we'll bring some more out safely. Okay? You've done very well. How do you feel?"

"Bumpy," said Ingrid, her hand rubbing over the scarring on her ankle.

The doctor smiled.

"Do you feel safe?" she asked.

"Now?"

"Yes, now."

"Safer. My mother is here now."

Doctor Stedman had not heard Liz enter the front door but did not doubt Ingrid's hyper vigilance.

"Before you go, don't forget if anything comes up that you find you're struggling with, ring me. You have my mobile number."

"No."

"You don't have my number?"

"Yes, I do. Not talk on the 'phone."

"Oh, okay. Perhaps you can text?"

"Text?"

"Write me a message on the mobile phone."

"Write?"

"Maybe your mother can show you."

"My spelling is not good."

"That's all right. Spelling's not important; besides everyone spells badly while texting. Autocorrect makes sure of it."

"I have bank money now. I could buy the tiny phone for me."

Liz greeted them as they moved into the waiting room.

"Ingram has been refused bail," she blurted instead of hello, obviously relieved.

Whatever her meeting with Robert had revealed, it had certainly unnerved Liz some. Ingrid, perhaps fortunately, did not register her mother's lack of ease.

"We'll buy a texting 'phone now," she suggested.

"Sorry?" Liz asked, still distracted. Doctor Stedman saw her breathe in, shake thoughts away and focus her attention on Ingrid. "You want to buy a mobile 'phone?"

"Can I?" Ingrid asked.

"Yes. It's probably a good idea. But don't forget, it is your money. You don't need my permission to buy things you might want."

"And a dog."

"Well, maybe you do need my okay for that one. We'll see. How about this 'phone? Maybe I should get a new one too, mine's an absolute brick nowadays and the camera is crap."

"A camera?"

"A photo maker. You can take photos with mobile phones."

"Oh."

"We'll see you on Thursday," Liz said to Doctor Stedman. "Thanks."

"Enjoy your shopping and call me if you need me."

"Text," said Ingrid.

"Or text," agreed the doctor.

Ingrid quickly followed her mother, eager to busy herself away from the past, and, braced with intent, they pushed themselves out into the winter's cold and hurried towards the mall.

Ingrid lost some of her verve when they entered, as her senses were overwhelmed by the noise, visual and auditory.

"We can just go home," suggested Liz, to allow Ingrid the option of escape. Ingrid was resolute.

"No," she said. "I need money."

"You can use your card."

Ingrid said, "No." Again, still resolute. "I'm learning money."

"Okay, to the ATM."

At the machine Ingrid stood perplexed by Liz's question.

"How much money do you think you need to buy a mobile phone?"

"Dollars, not cents," answered Ingrid.

"Yes, that's right."

"Five dollars?"

"I wish," said Liz. "Think about how much we pay just to stream movies online, and you're going to keep the phone forever."

"The stream is twelve dollars a month, a 'phone is for life? It is twelve times fifty-two, times seventy years. $43,680?"

"Okay, I'll take your word on the mathematics, but no, a little less than that. How about we take $200 and we check out the provider contracts?"

"Okay, if you think that's enough."

Ingrid pressed the relevant numbers on the keypad and the cash, in fifties, spat out of the machine. Ingrid counted the notes and safely put them away in her wallet.

It was a good hour before Ingrid had made her careful choice of a mobile phone and contract. The pair left the mall carrying shopping bags, keen to be away. No stopping for their normal post-shopping coffee, impatient to be home and charge their purchases rather than themselves, they arrived breathless at the bus stop, to see the bus pull into traffic. Liz had chosen the same mobile, but a different colour.

"Pox!" wheezed Liz.

"Pox!" echoed Ingrid.

They sat on the warm, newly vacated seats to wait.

18

Chapter 18

Ingrid was looking forward to Spring and its promises, even with the knowledge that warmer weather might precipitate unwanted remembering. For now, she felt uncomfortable in socks, shoes, and the other accoutrements of Winter. So sewn in, and stifled, pushing around a so-so mood. There had been triggered within Ingrid the genesis of self awareness, and subsequently an annoyance at her 'self,' that an ordinary exercise, such as putting on a scarf, gave rise to a wobbly legged fear response. It wasn't as if she would strangle herself, not intentionally, but Ingrid's body reacted as though there were hands about her neck. Mind and body did battle and Ingrid seemed to lose, no matter.

For Ingrid, the simple pleasure of looking forward, to Spring, or to anything, was a novelty. Although she had to plough into the apprehension that anything good could be stolen first. Ingrid, on those days that found her a little unfixed, surfaced to herself playing 'what if?' What if she woke up and found herself still chained to that bed? With this thinking had Ingrid now put the idea out there? To be taken up by some deity of the unfair to be made true, made possible? What if he were alive?

"You will always be mine. I own you."

Liz was also looking forward to Spring. It was the season of renewal, rejuvenation and sudden fervency.

"I might tackle the Tupperware cupboard soon," she said, thinking aloud.

"Sorry?" Ingrid asked, not quite listening.

"The plastics' cupboard. It's gotten way out of control. Containers without lids, lids without containers. It's plastic pandemonium. I have to close the cupboard really quickly or they try to escape en masse."

Then, nearly suddenly, Ingrid had a grounded assumption. It hit her in a nice way that the reason worst-case scenes kept tramping heavily through her consciousness might be that she, for the first time, had something to lose. She had freedom, she had her mother, she had some learning now, and more to come, all of which could be expropriated. For the longest time, in those hard days of her growing, she'd had nothing to lose, except her life, and she would have gladly given that up to be away from him. Now she did have something to lose. She had something.

"Wow," Ingrid said, smiling in this revelation.

"I know," Liz agreed, but she was still talking about up plastic storage. "It's amazing how quickly these things get out of hand."

"Does having stuff always give fear of losing it?" Ingrid asked, trying to voice thoughts.

"Hmm, methinks you're not talking about kitchen storage. What'ya thinking about?"

Ingrid rocked a little, as she did when a little uncertain and inside grasped for words that would articulate her mind's shorthand.

"If," she began and then stopped. "When," she tried again. "No. Do you, when you get stuff, good stuff, do you get... Um, get scared that someone's going to take it?"

"Steal my things? A thief?"

"Yes, but no. Time takes a lot of stuff."

"Do you mean, if you're around long enough bad things will happen and you'll lose things that are important to you?" Liz asked, trying very hard to understand.

"Nearly. Um... I think, if I relax, it'll go. Lost"

"If you're meaning all this," Liz waved an arm vaguely about the room. "Won't last. You're right, it won't, but that doesn't mean that what happens next will be bad." Ingrid nodded, Liz continued, "I can understand the fear though, a long time ago something that was pretty much my world was taken."

"What?"

"You, ya doof!"

"Oh."

"But we can't live always expecting horrible things to happen. Because if you wait long enough bad or sad times occur. People die, you lose contact with friends, or things, but you have to try and enjoy the stuff you do have, when you have it, and that's bloody hard."

"Was it really bad when I was gone?" Ingrid asked, curious.

Liz looked at her daughter to gauge her mood and saw that Ingrid was not unduly disturbed or uncomfortable.

"Well," she said. "For the longest time I was really a mess. People kept reporting sightings of you. Then the Police thought they'd found you once, but it wasn't you. Hope and then no hope. And then it all grew quiet and I had to just learn to function and not give up in case you came back. A childless parent. It was pretty horrible. Nothing like you went through, but hard for me."

"I'm sorry," Ingrid said, sad.

"No, it wasn't your fault! Don't ever think that. You don't, do you?"

Ingrid shrugged.

"I don't know. My mind, it goes 'round."

"All sorts of thoughts?"

Ingrid nodded.

"If they get too much, share them. If you say things out loud sometimes they're easier to sort."

"Is that why you talk to yourself?"

"Hey! No. I talk to myself?"

"A little."

"Hmm. Might talk myself into making some lunch. Do you feel like soup, followed by roast lamb with rosemary, roast veggies and a salad?"

"Yum. Yes."

"That's a shame, 'cause we're having two-minute noodles... I should go grocery shopping this arvo."

* * *

"Crikey, that hill," Liz said as she exploded in through the front door, puffing. "I'm going to order online from now on."

Ingrid called from the kitchen, where she was ready to help pack away the groceries, "Sounds like a good idea."

"You should've come," said Liz entering the kitchen. "It was awful. Some sort of jumble sale at the church. People everywhere. Children, dogs, nannies with large handbags. Ten deep at the check-outs. Loud as."

"Yuck," said Ingrid. "You will be needing a beer."

"Yes, I will be wanting a beer. I'll just put my stuff away. Were you all right alone?"

"Yes."

"Good work."

"Well, looks like you've got the unpacking under control, I'll just go and get these shoes off, and then we'll have a beer together. Maybe outside if the sun stays shining."

Liz was soon back in comfy slippers.

"Am I the same as I used to be?" Ingrid asked as soon as Liz entered the kitchen.

"Crikey, I'm out of the room for a few minutes and I miss some sort of existential crisis."

"Beg your pardon?"

"What brought this on?"

"Am I the same? Is there a part of me, maybe my... What do you call it? My core, maybe, that stayed, as when you knew me... before?"

"Does a part of you feel the same?"

"I don't know, maybe. I forget who I was. If your core is... Damaged, can it be made back the same."

"I don't know, sweetie, we were both changed by what happened, but I think we're essentially the same people."

"I don't remember who I was, but I want to give you back what was taken. Not me broken. But the first Ingrid."

"Hon, I still see the old Ingrid in you at times. She's not gone but grown. I loved you then, and I love you now."

"Even if my core is broken?"

"Even if, but I think you'll find that your core is okay. You're still as gentle and sweet as you always were, and that shows courage and strength. You could have easily become... I don't know, hard, bitter and horrible."

"I would like to give you back who was taken."

"You have, and more. Remember, it was not your fault. You're not responsible for what those poisonous men did. Can I have a hug?"

Ingrid looked fleetingly dubious but then complied.

"And then a beer?" she suggested.

19

Chapter 19

After a dismal cold snap, Spring vividly appeared. It was the kind of weather that might grow a poet lyrical but Liz had her head in the kitchen cupboards, for the planned Spring cleanup and Ingrid had her head in the book she was struggling to finish for school.

"What's O-B-F-U-S-C-A-T-E?" She spelt out, entering the kitchen.

"What? Oh, obfuscate," answered Liz, from within the cupboard.

"Obfuscate? What's it mean?" Ingrid asked, putting her head almost into the cupboard to question.

"To confuse or obscure."

"I know confused, but what is obscure?"

"Obscure can have a few different slants." Liz explained, muffled in the cupboard. "In speech it's something not clearly explained, or nor easily understood, but it can also mean indistinct, or kind of unfocused. Or if it's an obscure person..."

"Why can't they just say what they mean?" Ingrid complained, flinging the paperback, to slide flapping across the kitchen table.

"To cause obfuscation," Liz said, rising from the cupboard, and pulling off her rubber gloves. "Let's have a coffee and then you can help me put all this stuff on the floor back in."

"Okay."

"Hey, don't get discouraged by one word. Really, obfuscate is kind of an obscure word. Think of the twenty million words you've already read."

"Some of them weren't easy either, and this is just a teenager book. I'm the dumbest in the class."

"You fucking retard! Answer me when I'm fucking talking to you!"

He wrenched at the chain, and the shackle bit deep into ankle as the dark ascended to meet the fall.

"Ingrid? Ingrid? You okay? Sit down. You look very pale."

Liz pulled out a kitchen chair and steered without touching Ingrid into it. Ingrid was shaking or shaken and seemed beyond words.

"I'll get you a water," Liz proposed, and on the turn to the sink promptly kicked and scattered the saucepans and lids, waiting to be re-housed, about the kitchen floor loudly. "Shit!" she said above the din, and then she saw a hint of a smile from Ingrid and felt a lessening of crisis.

With a glass of water for both of them, Liz sat at the table with Ingrid.

"A flashback?" she asked.

Ingrid nodded affirmative.

"Do you need anything? Do you want to talk about it?"

"I... I..." Ingrid stumbled. "I need it to stop."

"I know, hon. But it's a little easier." Ingrid looked dubious and Liz elaborated. "A month or two back a flashback could so overwhelm you that you'd end up in the hospital."

"This, it... It wasn't a bad one."

"But you made it through. Not even a sedative. Give yourself some credit. "

"I get scared."

"I know, sweetie. But think of yourself as one of those wind-up toys. For nearly fifteen years you were getting wound up, or keyed up, tighter and tighter. A less tough toy would just snap, but now you're safe to run it out. You can't just let it be because you say, *that's it*, you've got to let your workings all unwind again safely. Know what I'm saying?"

"What's, what's a wind-up toy?"

"Oh, bollocks, I thought that was a good analogy. Let's say, you're a yo-yo and the string... "

"No, let's say, you're a yo-yo. What about co... Coffee?"

"I can do this, let's say... "

"I... I'll whip cream for the top."

"Okay, you win. I'll pick up this mess. You be the barista."

"That is the coffee person?"

"Yep. Crikey, look, one of the saucepan lids nearly made it to the backdoor."

* * *

"Look what I found at the shops."

"Groceries?" asked Ingrid.

"Yes, them too. But tah-dah!" Liz pulled a metal mouse with a key in its back from her shopping bag.

"What is it?

"It's an old-fashion wind-up toy. When I went to get your prescriptions, I saw it in the chemist shop's window."

"Let's say, you're a yo-yo... Although, it is cute."

Liz had finished winding the toy and let it skitter across the floor, its key still in, rotating.

"It's for you."

"Thanks, Mum. I... I do like it."

* * *

Liz 'phoned the doctor's to talk the receptionist.

"Has Ingrid arrived for her appointment?"

"Yes, Mrs Brenner. She's in with the doctor now."

"Thank God. Was she all right when she arrived?"

"She looked quite pale, but she was verbal."

"Only the school just rang to say she was absent today and they were worried. And then I was worried. I saw her onto the morning bus."

"Well, she's here safely. Should I interrupt the session and let the doctor know of the absence, do you think?"

"Might be an idea. Could you also ask Ingrid to wait for me there? I'm a little nervous of her catching the bus home alone."

"Okay, but I'm sure she'll be fine."

"I know. It's more for me. I'll be on the next bus."

"Excuse me, Ingrid." said Dr Stedman, when the 'phone on her desk buzzed. "Yes? Yes... Okay, I see. Thanks, Jo."

Ingrid was sitting on the floor, sometimes she it found more comfortable than the boofy lounge chairs in the doctor's office. The doctor returned to the sofa she'd been sitting on and returned her clipboard to her lap. "Sorry," she apologised.

"Is okay."

"Is it?"

"Sorry?"

"I'm told you didn't attend classes today."

"Oh."

There grew an elongated silence, punctuated by traffic noises seeping through from outside of the window, cracked to allow in some unconditioned air.

"What happened today?" asked the doctor, sliding down to join Ingrid on the floor. "It's not like you to miss your English lessons."

Ingrid began to shake, unperturbed, Dr Stedman pushed forward. "Stay with me. You are safe here. What happened?"

"The bus," began Ingrid, hesitant but willing. "Got into town early... "

Prompted, "Yes?"

"In the park, near the Library. He... I thought I saw him."

"If you ever tell anybody about me I will fucking kill you! And I'll know."

"Who, Ingrid?"

"I always keep the gun loaded and that bullet is for fucking you dead, retard."

"He put the gun... He put the gun up... Inside me."

"Today?" asked the doctor, confused. Ingrid was rocking. Pale and afraid.

"No," she answered, infuriated at not finding the right words. "No. Before... But today I saw him."

"Saw who?"

"If you tell anyone, you're fucked!"

"I was fucked anyway."

"Sorry? Ingrid, take some deep breaths. Now, who did you see today?"

"I can't say his name. Fuck me!"

"Ingrid, it's okay. Did you see your kidnapper today? Is that who you saw? Ingrid?"

"I thought it was him. Then I disappeared."

"Sorry?"

"When I woke up I was down at the waterfront. He was gone, and my 'phone said it was three hours later."

"What were you doing down at the waterfront?"

"I don't know, I... I just woke up there."

"Were you alone?"

"There was an old lady near me."

"But you were by yourself?"

"Yes."

"How did you get to the seawall, to the waterfront?"

"I don't know."

"You just woke up there?"

"Yes."

"Were you lying down?"

"What? I don't know. No. I was sitting on the edge.'"

"The seawall?"

"Yes."

"Don't be cross; I was just trying to work out what happened."

"I don't know. I saw him, then I woke up at the seawall."

"But you're not sure it was him?"

"No."

"Do you think he's dead?"

"Not here," Ingrid answered, tapping herself on the chest. "He's always still here."

"You mean the flashbacks? But do you, in reality, think he's dead?"

"That day," began Ingrid, struggling.

"The day they found you?" the doctor prompted.

"Yes. I... I saw him go towards the building. His friend... "

"Jon Ingram?"

"No."

"Go on."

"The building. Very loud. Ringing."

"It blew up?"

"Yes."

"There was fire."

"You're pretty sure 'he' blew up in the building?"

"Yes."

"So, it couldn't have been him you saw this morning?"

"No. I don't know. I thought... Maybe. I don't know!"

"It's okay. You've done well today. How do you feel?"

"Scared. He will kill me."

"Not if he's dead."

"No. There is my mum!" Ingrid said, surprised.

"Okay. In that case, I'll see you in two days. Text me if you need me, or if you 'disappear' again."

"Okay."

"I might just have a quick chat with you and your mother. She's probably worried. We won't take a minute."

"Okay."

The doctor opened her office door and called Liz into the room. Liz entered, uncertain, timid.

"Are you all right?" she asked Ingrid.

"Yes."

"Good."

"I'm glad you came in, Liz," the doctor said, retaking her seat on the lounge.

Ingrid, this time, sat in an empty chair, foregoing her place on the floor, sensing a more formal turn in the mood.

"I gather, you were a little worried when Ingrid didn't show for class?"

"Yes," answered Liz, with a smile of reassurance toward her daughter. "It gave me a bit of a shock."

"Me too," Ingrid said.

"It wasn't planned? What happened?"

"If Ingrid would allow me. This morning, on her way to class," the doctor explained to Liz. "She thought she saw her kidnapper." Liz paled, the idea of him unthinkable. "This is a concern, of course," Dr Stedman continued. "But I'm also alerted to the possibility that Ingrid experienced a dissociative fugue."

"A what?" asked Liz, still whirling from events, darkly nauseated.

"A dissociative fugue is an unawareness of one's own identity, usually coupled with a flight of some sort."

"Loss of identity? Like amnesia?"

"In a way. It's not due to physical injury, more a psychological one. Ingrid lost time and found herself down by the water hours later."

"Was it him? Do you think it was him and he took her down there?" Liz asked, afraid for child.

"No. Ingrid's reasonably sure he didn't survive the blast. Seeing a man that looked like him prompted her to flee physically and mentally."

"But she's okay now?"

"Yes," Ingrid answered for herself. Liz smiled at her, relieved.

"But I'd like you both to be aware of the lost time and let me know if it happens again."

"Okay."

"All right, I'll see you in two days, Ingrid."

"Okay."

Both Ingrid and Liz were still rather shaken when they left the doctor's rooms, wary perhaps of aftershock.

20

Chapter 20

A 'phone call surprised Liz, barely awake; she reached for the telephone on her bedside table. All phone calls surprised Liz, really.

"Hello, it's Robert; I didn't wake you, did I?" the detective asked. "I know it's early."

"No, no, I've been awake for seconds now. Possibly even minutes."

"Sorry, I wanted to ring you before work. As you know, Major Crimes has Ingrid's case now, so I'm not bending any rules if I see you," Robert faltered. "Um, socially," he added.

"Oh," said Liz, still too sleepy to be helpful.

"Could I come up to the Coast, and drop in on you? And Ingrid? I'd like to see how you're both getting along."

"We're getting along fine, but yes, a visit would be nice. When do you have time off?"

"I'm off Sunday and Monday this week."

"Okay, why don't you come up, say, for lunch on Sunday? If it's a nice day, we could walk down and have fish and chips on the waterfront."

"Sounds great. About eleven then?"

"Lovely."

Liz put the handset back in its charging cradle and flumped back on the pillows.

"Well," she said.

Ingrid, she could hear, was up and hunter gathering in the kitchen.

"I can't lie around here all day. I've got to do something about my hair... Before Sunday."

Vanity is a great motivator, and the hairdresser's appointment Liz had been lazily postponing for months was duly made.

"Would you like to get your hair done, too?" Liz asked Ingrid later that day.

"What is 'done' mean?" Ingrid asked.

"You know, cut, and maybe a colour put in."

"Cut?"

"She's got fucking head lice. Hold her while I shave her hair off. Fucking keep still, bitch, I'm doing this for you! May as well do your pubes while we're at it. Don't want no crabs. Make her look young again, too, eh? No, this is no good; help me tie her to that chair. Fuck! You're fucking useless! I'm gunna knock you to next week, you stupid bitch."

"Here, I've brought you a Xanax. Are you okay, hon?"

Ingrid nodded yes, but took the tablet, shaking with a cold that came from within. Contrarily, the day outside shone warm.

"Would you like a throw rug?" Liz asked, although she, herself was sweating. She went to fetch the rug without waiting for an answer.

The blades are still in the bathroom, Ingrid thought, feeling their sharp edge call her.

"How about a nice warm shower?" Liz asked, as she wrapped the rug around her daughter's trembling body.

Invitation. The bathroom. The blades.

"No!" said Ingrid, forceful. "Yes. No," indecisive in predicament. "Yes, I shower." Sometimes the fight just leaves. The blades called again. Release.

It wasn't until the blood that Ingrid really woke to what she was doing in the shower. She cursed herself. Cursed the blades. Saw them abandoned red on the shower floor. Saw the blood. Saw the failure. She used a face washer to staunch the blood flow from her arm and when the blades were re-hidden, a secret in the vanity cabinet drawer, Ingrid dressed, still holding the face washer over the bleeding gash. She would have to tell her mother, but she felt this would wound her mother too. There was so much blood, it couldn't be ignored. Maybe death would be simpler?

"Ingrid? You okay?"

No hiding now.

"No."

"Can I come in?"

"Yes."

"Oh, shit! Okay, let's have a look. Feel like a trip to the hospital?"

"Don't lock me up."

"No. No. Just stitches. Do you feel all right? Not dizzy?"

"I'm okay."

"Maybe just down to the medical centre then. You sit while I'll call a cab. Hold that cloth tight."

"I'm sorry."

"No, no, it's not your fault. You have so much inside. Some of it has to get out somehow. But you've really got to find a better way, okay? I love you."

Three words.

Ingrid's heart broke.

* * *

That afternoon, sewn up and mending a little, Ingrid sat listening to a talking book, passing the time studiously until her mother returned from the hairdresser. She was supposed to be following the recorded words in her own copy of the novel, sitting open on her lap, but her mind was unsettled. Grinding awkwardly from the book at hand to her thoughts and back. She wanted so much to be unbroken for her mother, for Doctor Stedman, for herself, and he kept grabbing her like a rip, a devious undertow, dragging her out of her new life to the past, where she couldn't swim. Carrying her enemy within, making her heavy. Making her lose time. Making her bleed. How could she get his malevolent self out of her present-day and leave him dead in history?

"To erase him I'd have to erase me," Ingrid said aloud.

No. She was too tired. Ingrid closed the book and turned off the library app. Tea? No. For some reason there had to be two for tea. Coffee? No. Beer? Maybe. Scream? Want to.

There was a clattered noising at the entry and Liz tumbled in askew through the front door.

"Bollocks!" she said.

"What's wrong?"

"I tripped on the doormat again. For goodness sake, it's not like I don't know it's there. Need a sign on the gate, *beware of the bloody mat.*"

Ingrid smiled and went to greet her mother.

"Your hair is good."

"Thank you," Liz accepted.

"You remind me of you."

"Sorry?" Liz asked for elaboration, as they walked into her room together so that she could throw off her street shoes.

"Umm. You look like who I used to know."

"Oh, you mean, with less grey, I look more like how you remember?"

"Yes."

"Good-o. I'll take that as a compliment."

"You do look good."

"Thank you. When you're feeling better, maybe you could get your hair styled, do you think? It can be quite therapeutic."

"He shaved my head."

"Oh, hon."

"My ear. Cut the bit off the top. See?"

"Jesus! I hadn't seen that before. Your hair usually covers it. Death was too easy an out for that freaking bastard! But thank you for telling me. It's good for me to know some of the stuff you've been through."

"Good?" Ingrid was surprised.

"Yes, hon. Then I can understand more. Know why you're triggered. Know how I can help."

"Oh."

"What's the matter?"

"I don't want to be a... a, the word? Load, a load? The burden."

"You're not a burden! Never were, never will be. You are my child. Besides, when I'm old and infirm, you could be looking after me."

"I'm not good at cooking."

"If you're lucky I might lose all of my teeth and you can just put everything in the blender and press mush." Liz flopped on the lounge. "How's your arm?"

Ingrid shrugged; she wanted to be far away from the morning. Disown her damage and float with a little peace on denial, above the undertow.

Liz saw and changed the subject as she slipped off her scuffs and wriggled her toes in freedom, "I was looking at the front garden on my way in, it needs some work."

"Before Sunday?" Ingrid asked.

"Is that you teasing? Well, yes, I would like it to look nice before Robert visits. Can't have him being swallowed by privet on his way up the path."

"No," said Ingrid, not sure what privet was, but not wanting anyone swallowed on the front path.

"Look at the time! Getting me to look half-way decent at the hairdresser's takes forever these days. I guess the garden can wait until tomorrow now. Hmm, might give myself a facial instead. Hey, do you want to do some girlie stuff with me? Put on a face mask, have a manicure? Kick back with a movie or something? Or did you finish reading those chapters for school?"

"No."

"Well, maybe we can listen to it together. It's been a hundred years since I read *Great Expectations*. Is it giving you the pip?"

"Ha, ha."

"All right, no more jokes. To the bathroom. Time for a face scrub."

In the pursuit of beauty, the two women buffed away the rest of the day, as Pip met Miss Havisham.

* * *

That evening the phone rang again, and Liz was surprised again. It was Robert for a second time.

"A friend of mine's dog has not long ago had a litter. You were asking about the dog from Peats Ridge not long back for Ingrid. Would she like a puppy? They're fox terriers and cute as."

"Oh, I've been stalling on that, but I guess she'd probably love one."

"I don't have to bring one. I just thought I'd ask."

"No. No, it might be good for her to have something that's solely her responsibility. She needs to feel that she's not always the one being cared for. No, it's a good idea. Bring one up."

"Any preference for sex? They've had all their shots. There's two girls and a boy."

"I don't know. Pick one that you think is fearless. We don't need a shaking mass of neurosis around here. That's my job."

"I'm sure it's not. But I'll do my best. Are you going to tell Ingrid or will we surprise her?

"I think it'll make a nice surprise for her. She's already in bed. She's had kind of a rough day."

"Sorry to hear that."

"Good days, bad days, that's life."

"Well, I'll see you on Sunday and hopefully that'll be one of life's good days."

"I'm sure it will be. See you then."

21

Chapter 21

Sunday dawned fine fish and chips weather. Ingrid moved her morning coffee to the backyard and sat in a sunbeam. Brilliant was the sky, all blue and daubed with fluffy clouds like a four-year old's painting. She thought how it seemed so generous and profound from the perspective of freedom. A sky like this, back when she sat chained to a tree, had merely backlit captivity, a view seep from the unobtainable. Just a part, for her, of the boxed in landscape. Now she could relax and take it in, the openness, deeply.

"Good morning, my child," said Liz, exiting the house, holding her own coffee. "Can I join you, or would you rather be alone?"

"Good morning, my mum. You can join."

Liz dragged a lawn chair into Ingrid's sunbeam, slopping coffee on the courtyard pavers as she went.

"Pox. I need my caffeine. Thought I might do some more to the front yard before I shower."

"Aren't you done? Can I help?"

"Sure. You have excellent weeding skills. That garden at the front side has more weeds than plants. We shall attempt to rectify the balance."

"Yes."

They sat in comfortable silence the two, enjoying the morning and their coffees preparatory to garden toil. Eventually the sunbeam moved and so reluctantly did they.

"What would you like on your toast?" Liz asked.

"Nothing thank you. No toast, I'm not hungry."

"You should eat."

"I will. Later. I'll start out the front."

"Mind your stitches. Don't do anything strenuous."

"I don't know what that means, but I'll take it easy."

"That's pretty much what it means. I'll be out there shortly."

Soothing became the repetition of movement and a pile of weeds arose beside Ingrid in a mangled wilting cluster. She whistled, a little tunelessly, to help keep thoughts satisfactorily absent.

"Good going, my garden minion," said Liz as she came into the yard. "Our work here is nearly done."

"Minion?"

"Slave."

"Okay."

Their companionable silence softly re-descended, punctuated occasionally with Liz's 'oomphs' as she pulled out exceptionally stubborn weeds.

"Crikey! Look at the time. I'd better go and have my shower and put my street face on before our visitor gets here," Liz said, straightening slowly as one does after a score or so years of back ownership.

"Too late," said Robert behind her.

"Well, pox."

"Sorry, the M1 was a surprisingly easy run this morning. I could drive around the block?"

"Okay," said Liz. "By the state of me, about thirty-seven times around should do it."

"You look fine. How about you do your thing while Ingrid helps me get some stuff from the car?"

Ingrid looked perplexed and hesitant.

"It's all right, sweetie," Liz put in. "You'll like what's in the car. I promise."

"Okay," said Ingrid, dubious but willing.

Liz scooted indoors, and Ingrid followed the policeman to his car.

"A puppy! You have a dog?"

"No. You have a dog. It's for you."

"Me?!"

"You want to hold him, while I get his stuff?"

"Yes."

"Here you go. He's a squirmy little bugger."

Once safely through the gate, Ingrid put the wriggling one down and he rushed to a bush and peed. And peed.

"Thank God, that didn't happen in the car," said Robert, following Ingrid on the path, carrying two bowls, a leash and other puppy paraphernalia. "He must store water like a camel."

The pup began joyfully exploring the yard. Darting from one smell to another in a drunk with excitement zigzag.

"Thank you," Ingrid said, softly, shyly.

"You're welcome. I'll go inside and put this stuff down. Let you two get acquainted."

Ingrid flopped to the ground and immediately the puppy was upon her, tail wagging, exuberance emanating from his very paws. He licked her face, cleansed her a little of the deep hurt within, and Ingrid smiled, actually feeling the delight.

"What are we going to call you?" she asked.

The puppy slid off but clambered straight back onto Ingrid's outstretched legs. He flopped content in her lap, chewing on her wriggling fingers. Happy and trusting.

"Well, he is a cutie," called Liz from the front door. "Bring him in and let's see what he thinks of our home."

The puppy rolled off as Ingrid made a move to stand and he positioned himself beneath every foot fall as they tripped their way inside. Liz and Robert were sitting at the kitchen, coffee and biscuits between them like chess pieces.

"Coffee's made," said Liz to Ingrid, but Ingrid dropped to the floor to play with the dog some more. "What are you going to call him?"

"I don't know," Ingrid answered.

"Bear in mind, not to use your favourite name. I read somewhere that apparently couples are finding that when they have their first born, the dog already has the good name... How about Woozel?"

"Had that ear marked for my first child," Ingrid replied, deadpan.

"He's a bit of a gonk," Robert said.

"Casey Woozel Gonk the First," announced Ingrid.

"Classy, but not pretentious," said Liz in agreement, she raised her mug in toast. "Why Casey?"

"Because he's a bit of a head case. Like me."

They watched as Casey drank some water, given this, Ingrid led the puppy quickly outside to the backyard before the water had time to reach his other end and leak out.

"Ingrid looks so much better than when I first met her. You've done wonders," Robert said.

"I've done very little. She's the survivor."

"Don't sell yourself short. Yes, she's a survivor, but you've given her a place to gently heal. She never would have found that in a hospital somewhere."

"She still cuts herself."

"You said yourself, the damage was done over a decade, why expect it to be repaired in a few years? Some of the older guys at work are still struggling with what happened to them in Vietnam and that was over thirty years ago. It's all still very fresh for Ingrid."

"I know. I just want her to be okay."

"She made a joke earlier, about her first child. She wouldn't have been able to do that a year ago."

"I know," Liz cheered up immediately.

"She has your sense of humour."

Liz grinned. "Hard to believe I could be a grandmother one day."

"I thought the medical report said Ingrid wouldn't be able to have kids?"

"What?!" Liz was so obviously stunned, daring to dream, she'd let her guard down. "Nobody told me. Does Ingrid know? Shit."

"I'm sorry. Probably wasn't my place to say anything. I just assumed they'd told you."

"Well, somebody should have! Can I get a hold of these reports?"

"I imagine her treating doctor has a copy. The hospital certainly has them on file. They conducted all the tests for us."

"I've a good mind... "

"Yes, you do, but don't go blundering in there half cocked. Bureaucracy takes delicate handling. They'll put a wall up if they think you're hostile."

"Fuck. So, he damaged her so much inside, that she can't have children?" The tears Liz thought she had let go, arrived back, fresh and unbidden. "I want to kill him."

"Yes, me too. But let's put it aside, just for now. I think you should talk to the doctors about the reports."

"Where do I put all this anger? How does Ingrid stay sane? Fuck."

"I'll get on the blower tomorrow and see why nobody thought to discuss any of this with you... Are you okay? Talk about blundering in. I did a fair job of that myself."

"I'll be fine. It's Ingrid, I worry about. This'll be yet another blow for her."

"You never know. She might already know. Her doctor may have discussed it with her."

"But the joke about her first born?"

"She said first child, not necessarily first born."
"You're such a policeman. Any other observations?"

"Yes. I like your hair."
* * *

As morning ticked over to afternoon the trio, plus dog, set off towards the waterfront. A cooler bag holding a bottle of wine and three glasses, mildly clinked their progress down the hill. The only dilemma for the afternoon, what type of fish to eat.

"It smells. I will wait over here with Casey. Away from all these people."

"Here, can you mind this?" Robert asked, handing Ingrid the wine bag.

"Yes."

There was quite a queue in the fish and chip shop. So Ingrid planted herself beneath a tree for the wait, Casey climbing all over her.

"Nice dog."

Ingrid froze, panicked. "I... I don't... talk to strangers."

"Fair enough, jeez, I was just admiring your dog. What are you, five?"

The man walked off, indignant. Ingrid fumbled into her pocket for a Xanax but stopped. *No. I am okay.* Her heart thudded a beat of fear and she felt the familiar nausea. *Maybe, just a half.* She swallowed a half tablet, quickly. "Might not talk to strangers, but to myself... I'm crazy," she told Casey. He licked her, happy. "You like crazy, huh?"

Half an hour later, Liz and Robert emerged from the crowded shop, smiling, talking together. Ingrid watched until they were quite close then moved her eyes away, feeling intrusive.

"Sorry, that took so long."

"It's okay. Casey pooed and I cleaned it up."

"Shame I missed that," Liz said.

"A man spoke to me."

Liz shot her a glance of concern. "That okay?" she asked.

"I had half a Xanax."

"Oh. But you're doing all right?"

"Yes. I said, I don't talk to strangers."

"Good on you," Robert said, smiling. "Men have to learn about personal space and boundaries."

"Shall we move further from the shop?" Liz asked. "Closer to the bridge, maybe? People don't often walk around that far."

"Sounds good," Robert agreed. "I bought Casey a bottle of water. He's too young to drink alcohol."

"Thank you."

Ingrid took the bottle and put it in the cooler.

"Let's blow this joint," said Liz. "I need chips immediately. With chicken salt. And lemon."

They all picked up the pace, eager.

"Tartare sauce," Liz continued.

"Stop it," Robert said. "I'm suddenly starving."

"That palm tree, there," Liz said, pointing at their goal. Shade, a bin nearby, uninterrupted view of the water and there appeared to be no gulls.

"Perfect."

The picnic was had. Of course, sea gulls did turn up, without invitation.

"How do they know? Shoo!"

"I think they send out a spotter gull on reconnaissance and he flies back to give them the co-ordinates of the humans showing eating behaviours," answered Robert.

"Funny, they don't seem that sophisticated," Liz said, watching one gull squawking like a banshee.

"Wish I could fly," said Ingrid.

Liz looked at her daughter, relaxed, lazily popping a chip in her mouth, passing her new puppy a piece of fish. Having come so far.

"You will," said Liz, speaking, dreaming, metaphorically for her child.

22

Chapter 22

Night, the unlit portal for dark dreams to slither insidiously past the sleeping guard. Waking cold from a nighttime sweat, uncomfortably saturated pyjamas and damp sheets, tiredly Ingrid pulled up the covers about her neck and trembled back to sleep.

When daylight seeped through the squinting venetian blinds she woke unrested with nothing left of the dream but the branded imprint of pain, and a pervasive fear wafting over her like an ugly perfume. Ingrid hated starting the day this way, already churning, depleted, nervous. Damp to the bone. She pulled the wettish sheets from the bed to the sounds of Casey at her door eager to greet. She smiled a little at this. On the first opening of the bedroom door he burst in all pupped up, bouncy and exuberant. Ingrid succumbed, dropping to the floor to be walked upon, licked and chewed.

"Come on. Let's get you some brekky."

"What day is it?" asked Liz entering the kitchen confused with sleep, and lack of coffee.

"Tuesday, November 27th, 7:45am," answered Ingrid from the dog's bowls where she poured dog biscuits for the hungry pup.

"Ta... Rough night?" Liz had spied the pile of sheets on the laundry floor.

"I guess."

"Coffee?"

Ingrid nodded agreement, too tired for words. She ambled out through the back door and Casey rushed after her, biscuits falling from his mouth and he set about peeing hello to the outdoors.

"You okay?" Liz asked, bringing out the coffees, closing the screen door with a flip of her foot.

"I don't know," Ingrid answered after thought, watching Casey run amongst the shrubs in search of something. "I want to be okay."

She joined Liz at the wooden table, sliding along the bench seat until she was hit by a sunbeam.

"Hmm," said Liz in a 'go on' kind of way.

Ingrid did, "It's... It's confusing. My inside... I want... It's good. I'm free. I'm with you. There is a puppy. But..." the sentence disappeared.

"But?" Liz prompted.

Ingrid struggled. "I am okay, but I'm also not okay."

"Hmm," repeated Liz. "A sort of a psylogical dilemma? It might just be left over from your nightmares. You did have one last night?"

Ingrid nodded, feeling the dream's shadowy intimation touching her still.

"It might wear off," Liz continued. "Could just be a bad start to the day."

"Yes."

"Well, I guess it can only improve from here."

"Is that some of those 'famous last words' I read about?"

Liz smiled, "I hope not. I'm not ready to shuffle off yet. Besides you have to wear flowery nanny slippers to shuffle off properly and I'm sticking with Ugh boots for a few more years yet."

"Shuffle off?"

"A euphemism for dying."

"Oh. There seems to be a lot of euphemisms for dying."

"Yes, but I heard somewhere that vomit has the most substitute synonyms in English."

"Vomit?"

"Yeah, you know, puke, hurl, upchuck, spew... "

"I get it."

"Heave, Technicolor yawn, ralph... "

"Okay, okay, keep it up and I'll regurg my coffee."

"Cheer you up some?" Liz gave a grin.

"Some. In a queasy kind of way."

"Well, you better go and get some breakfast et cetera or you'll miss your bus."

"I'm not really hungry."

"You have to eat."

"You're the one who brought vomit up, if you'll pardon the expression."

"No, seriously, you look like you're losing weight again. Have a shower first, then you might feel more like it."

"Okay, but don't nag."

To erase him, she would have to erase herself.

* * *

The bus was late. Ingrid had to sprint up the hill towards the language school. As she jogged she heard a male voice call her name from behind. Afraid, she ran faster, not turning to identify the caller.

"He's dead. He's dead," she told herself, to soothe, as a running mantra.

Tiredness reached her before the corner and Ingrid slowed her aching calves to a brisk walking pace and crossed the road to the school. Upon seeing a group of her classmates congregating loudly, happily at the entrance she slowed, hoping they would enter before she reached the door. Normally Ingrid would wait until they'd moved inside but the fear of what was behind kept her moving forward. *He's dead. He's dead.*

But the current took Ingrid. Past the entrance to the school and toward the town library. She did not struggle but let herself float effortlessly to the doors to be swallowed inside, before the resilience ebbed from her and weak, she dropped into a chair ensuring a wall behind her and the entrance in direct sight. She watched. *He's dead. He's dead.* Waited. Tension eased as time brought no-one but an elderly couple through the doors, string bags empty, ready to fill with books.

'I'm late for school,' Ingrid thought, but the idea of walking into the classroom, everyone looking on curiously as she made her stumbling apologies to the teacher, was easily discouraged. Maybe she could slip in during the noise of morning break.

The elderly couple were in the large print section nattering quietly over choices. Ingrid searched out her library card and went to join them. She liked the large print; it seemed to make the words appear simpler. Like a children's reader. After choosing one book, Ingrid grabbed another thicker, heavier novel. If some man was calling out her name, pursuing her, he could see how a couple of large print Anne Tyler's swung at him in a backpack felt across the side of the head. *He's dead. He's dead.* Armed, Ingrid left the library and headed back to the school, the weight of her bag reassuringly digging her painfully, pointedly in the back as she walked.

As she neared the school she saw her mother, anxious, at the entrance.

"Ingrid! What happened?" Liz asked. "One of the teacher's said he called out to you but when you reached the school you ran off like a scared rabbit. They rang me. Why didn't you answer your mobile?"

Liz was having trouble keeping the strain from her voice.

"I'm... I... Sorry."

"As long as you're all right. You're all right?"

"Yes."

"I put my phone on silent ready for school."

"Okay."

"I... Why did they ring you? I'm... I am grown up."

"I guess they were worried."

"They probably wouldn't ring Kim's mum, or... Or Luan's mum, if they... If... If they saw them speed off."

"Ingrid, a lot of people care about you. They think you've been hurt enough. They don't want any more harm to come to you. That's all. They're not trying to baby you."

"That's good. But you saw. I was coming back. They alarmed too soon. I am grown."

"I know. It's only because they care. Are you sure you're all right?"

"You worry. Too much."

Liz smiled. "Yes, I do. But I'm trying to cut down."

"I will go in now."

"Okay. See you when you get home after Doctor Stedman's. I love you."

"I love you too. Stop worrying."

"I'll do my best."

* * *

"It's quite normal that your flight responses kick in early," Doctor Stedman assured, on hearing of Ingrid's morning run. "You're trying to ensure that what happened to you as a child never happens again, and that's a good thing. You'll gradually learn to assess situations and react appropriately as time goes on."

"I don't want to... To run every time I hear... Some... My name loud. It's stupid."

"Don't be hard on yourself. I would've reacted the same way in your shoes. Congratulate yourself on finding a safe place when you felt in danger. You gave yourself a space to work out whether there was a threat and you were ready to go back to class. A few months ago, you might have been still running... And I would've been the one ringing your mother." The doctor smiled and Ingrid felt a little better about her flight. "Now, next week I'll be at a conference on Tuesday, do you want to come on Wednesday instead?"

"What's a conference?"

23

Chapter 23

Fighting, flighting, sudden jolts, rapid beats and Ingrid woke tired, wary, but not unhappy. Mornings were a new beginning, a potential something, filling with organised, controlled dreams, not the chaotic visions and sounds of the dark time. Ingrid finished school for the year and had enrolled in School Certificate courses to start in the new year, after an encouraging elbow from her teacher. For now, she could read for enjoyment and if she accidentally learnt something along the way, that was a bonus.

Some find a good night's sleep helped the ability to cope with bad days. For Ingrid it happened that good days helped her contend with ill-behaved night-time dreaming. Sometimes, a just right boiled egg with toast 'soldiers' in a row for breakfast pushed a bad night a little further away. But she could never tell.

"Jeez, mate, she's getting skinny. When d'ya last feed her properly?"

"I don't fuckin' know. She wouldn't eat a perfectly good steak the other night so I stopped feeding her good stuff. I'm not wasting food on her."

"You'll bloody kill her."

"Whatever."

Erase.

"Not hungry this morning, sweetie?"

"Not really."

"I'll do us a special lunch then."

"You don't have to."

"I feel like cooking. You want to come down to the butcher's with me later? Walk the dog?"

"Maybe."

"How 'bout we have ourselves a barbecue? I could marinate some chicken drumsticks. We can dine al fresco with the flies, in true Aussie style."

"We will have to drink beer."

"Yes, we will."

"Mmm."

"Can I hug you?"

"What?!"

"Can I hug you?"

"Why?"

"Because I want to."

"Why?"

"Because I love you, egg! There's a difference between good touch and bad touch, you know?"

"Yes. That's true, but somehow my... my sub... what is it? Con-sciousness?"

"Yes, sub-conscious."

"My sub-conscious makes it fire... makes it burn. I... I can't control it."

"We'll teach it to behave itself. One quick hug then I'll throw water on you."

"Are you taking the mickey?"

"A little. Come on, I'm growing old here."

They hugged. Liz walked away, satisfied, to bring fresh coffees. Ingrid tried to still her illogical heart, wondering why it always defied knowing, defied the pleading, to be so easily quickened into affliction. Would she always react this way to human touch, even the safest embrace of a mother? Dr. Stedman had said, eventually she would become desensitized, but that sounded a like becoming even deader inside. If Ingrid managed to switch off the triggering of bad reactions, would her fledgling ability to taste happiness be deactivated too? Would the day come when she wasn't reminded that she was damaged? Would she eventually stop asking herself these pesky questions? Would... would she turn into wood? No really, would she have to be a shutdown piece of driftwood to bear her mother's hugs? Blah, blah, blah.

"I'm taking Casey for a walk!" Ingrid called to Liz, feeling an urgent need to get away from herself. Casey was eager too, falling over his own busy feet to get to the front door. He, in haste, made it difficult for Ingrid to connect the leash to his collar, delaying their exit to the point of slapstick.

"Come on, already!"

The day was cheerful, all postcard and brilliant. Ingrid headed Casey down toward the waterfront so that he could chase seagulls and roll in salt encrusted smelly things. Skirting the tourist pocked yacht club surrounds; they wandered to the less populated point where an elderly cemetery nestled by the sea in still quietude.

* * *

"What happened?" Ingrid asked, as the nurse walked out of earshot.

"We were hoping you'd tell us," Liz answered.

"I don't remember."

Ingrid's tone was laced with a tired layered despondency. When each layer peeled off, all that remained underneath was an identical concentric surface despondency and she, left weary from the flaying. Right in the heart of this melancholy was him. Always. She never saw him coming.

"Hon, I know it's hard for you," Liz said. "But you've fought back from here before. What triggered this, is less important than how you go on from now."

Ingrid shrugged, too tired for optimism.

"How did I get here?"

"Well, as far as I know, you were acting strangely in the cemetery and someone called the Police. They got our home number off Casey's dog tag and rang me to say meet them here. I did. That was a week ago."

"A week? Why, why can't I re... remember an entire week?"

"The medications wouldn't help."

"I'm tired of being a fucked unit."

"You know I don't like that term."

"Sorry."

"They say I can bring Casey in for a quick visit, since he's still quite small."

"Can't I just go home?"

"Coupl'a days, sweetie. Just let them sort out your medication, talk with Doctor Stedman and such."

"Everything takes forever in this place."

"You know it's always about the next five minutes in here. If it can't be done in five, it slides further and further away, but I'm on it. I shall nag on your behalf."

"Thank you."

"We'll have you home in no time, hon. What about Casey, eh? Even though you dropped the leash, he stayed with you the whole time under that tree. Police and all."

"Tree?" Ingrid's equilibrium lurched precariously, swung ruthless, nauseous as it was with unannounced dark recall.

"Ingrid?"

"It's okay."

"No, it's not. What happened at the tree, Ingrid?"

"Thought I'd forgotten you, hey moron? Enjoy the storm out here? Well, you look cleaner anyhow. Jeez, the creek came up pretty high. Must've been wild. Come here. Do me while you're clean. Jack me off."

"If you can't tell me, try and tell Doctor Stedman. Okay, hon?" Liz said.

People, lay experts, say 'the best revenge, is a good life,' but I have no life at all, thought Ingrid in the hissing self-hatred that can suddenly fester, callously in search of weakness within institutional beige distractionless walls. In and out of this mental health facility, no job, always an erratic heartbeat away from breakdown. 'What life? What fucking life?' Are there always mountains? Up, down, depressions, fugues, anxiety - always something to get over. Always.

"Bah!" Ingrid spat the word angrily.

"What's up?"

"My bloody blood pressure."

"It gets better, you know that," comforted Liz, wanting so much to put her arms around her child.

"Yes, but I... I need a tantrum."

"Fair enough. How 'bout some extra-tasteless decaf to wash that tantrum down with?"

"Bleah."

"And so say all of us. I'll smuggle you in some real coffee tomorrow," Liz promised.

"You're such a rebel."

24

Chapter 24

Ingrid's despondency, like a king tide, took some time to abate. She felt submersed, drenched, heavy with an added lethargy born of the oppressive damp, the struggle to try and act in a way that the doctors would deem releasable. But mostly she felt too weary for fabrication and the doctors upped her anti-depressant medication and waited, while Ingrid, constrained by walls could do nothing but wait either.

Liz began to fear after some time that Ingrid might go permanently under.

"Book learning," her daughter said suddenly.

"Sorry?"

"I learnt so much stuff last year."

Liz prompted for explanation, "You did, but I'm still not getting you."

"And now... I... I find that the world really is flat."

Liz couldn't help but smile at her daughter's growing creativity with language.

"Ah, depression, now I understand," she said, hoping her own fear that Ingrid might plummet into an abyss of gloom deep as to not be able to scramble back out again, hadn't been accidentally showing and adding to her daughter's melancholy. "Don't be disheartened," Liz added for them both. "This is a brain chemistry thing. A physical thing. Your synapse whatsits are being little bastards and your beta-waves are just out of sync, that's all. They'll come good. It's not entirely psychological. I've probably said it before, and I'm now old enough to repeat myself ad nauseam in a forgetful but quaint manner, give your self time to heal physically too, hon."

"Yeah, yeah," Ingrid mumbled in a not heartened way.

"I smuggled in coffee, a baggie in my pocket. Gotta lock your handbags in lockers these days, before they let you through."

"They're trying to stop... stop... such, cont... contraband getting in."

"Let's go have some, enjoy the illicitness. I'm sure it'll add to the flavour."

* * *

Perhaps it was caffeine, for Ingrid was only under the monotony of hospital for another week. Things pass, like kidney stones, unpleasantly, painfully, followed it seems by an almost mania of immense relief.

"The air... it tastes different out here!" said Ingrid as they walked away on the happier side of the locked hospital doors.

"You bet. Casey's going to be so happy to see you, bouncy as you are today."

"It's release. Can we, what's the word? Splurst on a taxi?"

"Splurge, and yes."

Release. Ingrid had spent most of her life confined forcibly. Every release now must be a little victory. Every confinement a little loss. Shut now in a taxi, she rocked to soothe, to contain herself, to wait excitedly for home. The taxi driver eyed her, suspicious, watching in his rear-view mirror. Liz just grinned. The driver saw her and appeared hurried, sped and seemed relieved when he deposited them on the curb.

"Did... Did I make him nervous?" Ingrid asked, watching the car pull away as Liz fumbled through her handbag for the front door keys.

"Don't know," she answered. "Who cares? He was a plonker. A little rocking for me would be preferable to a drunk on the verge of heaving in the back seat of my cab any day. Besides, it may have been the silly grin of happiness on my face that gave him the heebies."

"What's a plonker?"

"A shit, hon. We're in! You better go and see to your dog. I'll see to your bag."

"Tah."

Ingrid rushed to the back door, more locks and then out into the backyard where there was a noisy, joyous reunion.

25

Chapter 25

"Don't die," Ingrid told her mother, sudden, emphatic.

"Well, hon, with my lack of prowess crossing busy roads, et cetera, that's not a promise I can make." Liz rose from the garden bed and stretched her back.

"I couldn't... I couldn't lose you again."

"Same, but I will die some day. What brought this on? Do I look unwell or something? Do I need to put my face on? I feel perfectly fine."

"No. It's this hospital thing. I... I don't know."

"You do. The words will come."

"You are the... the only... Nothing is solid... The drugs, the waking up and not remembering. Losing pieces of me. You are... "

"It's okay, hon. I plan to be around for quite a while."

"Solid, you are my only... base."

"I love you," Liz said simply.

For the first time, Ingrid initiated a hug and Liz, surprised, dropped the bucket of weeds she was taking to the green bin to the ground, dropped herself beside it and began to cry. Ingrid was horrified and she too sat down hurriedly on the grass beside her mother.

"I broke you?" she whispered, as Casey bounded in on the unusual scene, happy to have them both down at his level.

"No," Liz managed, pushing Casey gently aside.

"I'm sorry... sorr... " Ingrid was made distraught at the sight of her mother's tears. "Can I? Do something?"

"It's okay. I'm fine."

"You're crying."

"Tears are okay here," Liz said, composure returning. "It's okay, I know how bad it was for you, if you cried, but hon, tears are okay."

"But you're sad I hugged you?"

"No, no! On the contrary, it made me very happy. Casey, bugger off!"

"Will we go inside?"

Ingrid aided her mother in recapturing the weeds that had littered in the spill from the bucket. They packed up, wordlessly, for they knew words were soon coming and headed inside.

Indoors, Ingrid prepared coffee as Liz disappeared into her bedroom. She returned to the kitchen table carrying two boxes. The smallest was a box of tissues. Ingrid was stricken.

"Don't worry," said Liz, seeing her daughter's worried look. "I'm obviously feeling a bit raw today. These tissues are just in case."

"In case of what?" Ingrid asked, trying to hold at bay an unwelcomed touch of panic. It had stabbed her heart without warning, to see her mother cry. Coffees were brought to the table.

"In case we feel like waving tissues at each other in surrender." There was a tiny piece of harmless, teasing sarcasm in Liz's tone. "Crying is allowed in this house," she added with authority. "It's nothing to be afraid of."

"I'm sorry," said Ingrid, so easily hurt.

"Oh, sweetie, don't apologise. Just use all this as a lesson in learning to deal with feelings."

"I hate feelings."

"I know, hon. But if you shut them off, you might as well be dead."

"Maybe I am... already. I... I just didn't, haven't had the sense... to lie down."

Liz chose to ignore this remark. "Crying is what separates us from the animals," she added. "Now come and see what's in this other box. Bring biscuits. This needs biscuits."

Casey agreed with biscuits and rushed to the cupboard where his dog biscuits were kept.

"He's such a smart dog. Give him a treat, too," said Liz.

Ingrid pulled out the jar that contained dog treats and Casey went into happy paroxysms. Eventually she arrived at the table with a plate of assorted people's biscuits.

The lid was lifted from Liz's box with little ceremony, revealing a disordered world of keepsakes. Photographs, trinkets, Ingrid's infants school reports and other records of the past interwoven into a collection mess of remembrances.

"I really should sort this stuff," Liz said. "At least write on the back of the photographs for you."

"Is that me?" Ingrid asked, pulling out a coloured photograph of a small girl from the clutter of memorabilia.

"Let's see. No, that's me. First day of school."

"You were cute."

"There's a picture of you on your first day at school in a photo album, do you want to see it?"

"No, let's keep looking in this." answered Ingrid touching the box. "I don't remember school at all," she added with a little regret slipping into her tone.

"Junior school days aren't that memorable really. They become quite monotonous and all roll in together. I only remember embarrassing stuff really. Stuff that I'd rather forget anyway."

"Like what?"

"I don't know, like being teased, or walking out of the loo with the back of your uniform tucked into the top of your underwear. Fainting in assembly. Things like that."

"Did you do that?"

"I was a bit of a fainter. Still am really, if I have to stand in one spot without moving for too long."

"What about the underwear thing?"

"Fortunately, I don't remember if that was me or somebody else. Let's just say it was someone else."

Ingrid smiled, but then switched serious, "Were you teased?"

"Yeah, a little."

"Why?"

"Basically, because I was different. My parents were both from Finland and had an accent, so did I, until I began socialising with Aussie kids at school. And then there was the lunchboxes. No Vegemite sandwiches for me. I had to beg my mother for ordinary sandwiches like the other kids."

"Where are they now?"

"Who? My parents? They died quite a while ago."

"Oh."

"Here, this is them," Liz pulled a photo from a pile she'd been going through as they talked.

"They look happy," Ingrid observed.

"They were happy. It took a lot to bring them down, but they didn't stay down for too long."

"Not like me."

"That's not true. Hey, look here's you skiing for the first time. Look at that wide, wide smile."

Ingrid took the photograph from her mother and looked for a time at her younger self.

"I wish I remembered her," she said of herself wistfully, as if of a stranger she'd met fleetingly.

"Just because you don't remember her, doesn't mean she never was."

"Grow up, you fucking little bitch. Fuck! You fucking bite me again; I'll knock your fool teeth fair out of your fucking mouth. Grow up!"

"I guess she... She had to go... To save herself."

"You look sad," Liz observed. "It is a grief. To lose continuity. To lose memories. You are allowed to grieve."

"I stopped... I stopped fighting. If I... If I... I hadn't stopped."

"You'd probably be dead," Liz finished for her.

"It was a not large death, but she **is** gone," Ingrid said, pointing to her smiling small self.

"How does it make you feel?" asked Liz.

"No! No, feeling! Don't make... Make me do that."

"It's okay. It helps make you solid. You want solid, right? That's what you said. These photos are you. You are real. Solid."

"No. No." Ingrid pushed away from the table, almost toppling over Casey. "Shower... I need shower."

"No. I'm sorry! I pushed too far. Stay. We'll pack it up. Fuck!" swore Liz, as Ingrid rushed from the room. What had she been thinking, bringing out this box? This memorabilia. This past unobtainable to Ingrid. The shower was running, full. Ingrid's way of tears, of letting water flow. Liz packed up the box, leaving out the photo of Ingrid on her little skis, to stay on the kitchen table, a corner under the plate of biscuits, safe from the slight breeze.

As she passed the bathroom door with the box, she called, "Hon, you okay?" There was no answer, so she hurried to put the box back away in her wardrobe and returned quickly to the door.

"Hon?" The door was unlocked; Liz opened it a little. "Can I come in?" she called through the gap. "Hon?" The lack of answer proved too much for Liz and she invaded Ingrid's privacy.

Her child was sitting on the shower floor, naked, rocking, childlike, but held in the fingers of her right hand, a blade.

"No, hon," Liz whispered soothing, keeping the fear from her voice. "This was my fault, not yours. Don't punish yourself." Liz moved half into the shower cubicle, crouching beside her daughter. "Please give me the blade."

"I have to... to."

"No, you don't."

"To... to let it out."

"What out?"

Ingrid hit her own chest with her left hand, thumping hard. "This."

"Please, give me the blade. We can let it out another way. Please, hon."

Ingrid's mouth opened, but no sound came out. She rocked more fervently, still holding the blade. Blood had begun to seep, diluted by the shower water from her fingers to stream toward the drain.

"Give me the blade for now," softly ordered Liz. "I'll give it back in a few minutes, if you still need it. Please."

She pried Ingrid's fingers open and the blade fell. Liz picked it up, slicing herself a little, and placed it outside of the cubicle. Her child rocked, battling an anguish within herself, an anguish that Liz could not take from her. Ingrid thumped her arm, hard up against the tiled wall.

"No, hon."

Liz, crawling fully into the shower now, hugged her arms around Ingrid protectively; to contain her adult child's flying angry arms. Trapped in this manner, with no other outlet, Ingrid finally began to sob. They clung hard for some time, Liz's body screamed to be outstretched but she refused to relinquish her child to the inner turmoil so brutal. They remained folded together on the floor of the shower, quaking, wretched but consolidate. Eventually the sobbing eased. Liz could feel Ingrid's torment filled body was still not finished, but the water turned tepid, warning of the cold to come.

"Come on, hon. Time to get out."

Ingrid came gently, done and meek. She let Liz dry her shaking body and sat wrapped in a towelling robe on the closed toilet lid, rocking moderately now, while Liz stripped off her own wet clothing and dried off.

They both left the bathroom exhausted, weakness sending them straight to the kettle for coffee rather than dealing with wet clothes, bathroom mess or what was left of their emotions. Ingrid took a place at the table, and after a while picked up the photo Liz had left there, her skiing small smiling self, and then slid it protectively into her pocket.

26

Chapter 26

"There's nobody in my classes over twenty. I am old," Ingrid announced to Liz amidst a greeting as she arrived home from the college having braved the first full day back.

"Nobody?" Liz echoed.

"No. And there was nobody from last year, either. They, they were all strangers."

"Oh. Stranger than you?"

"What? Yes. No. Are you all right?"

"Yes, fine. What about a coffee? Then we can sit down and have a chat. Instant or real? Drop your bag."

"Real," Ingrid answered, letting her backpack slide off her shoulder to the floor. "But I'll get it. You sit down."

"No, no. I'll get the coffee. I haven't done much all day. Biscuit?"

Ingrid nodded the negative and said, "Are, are you sure?"

"Sure about what?"

Liz busied herself with her task and Ingrid watched from the table, curious, worried. Her mother still wore her ugh boots, as if her morning ritual of showering and changing out of her pyjamas to face the day was incomplete.

"About being all, all right," Ingrid said.

"I'm fine," Liz reassured, coming to the table with the fresh coffees. She placed them carefully on the table and sat down across from Ingrid. "Although, I do have a bit of a headache. I'll just get some paracetemol. Back in a tick."

Liz was up again quickly, and out of the room before Ingrid could comment. Casey came inside from the garden and bounded straight to the table when he realised Ingrid was home, trying in his over excited manner to get on her lap. She slid to the floor and they had a proper greeting, with hugs, pats and licks. Casey rolled onto his back and Ingrid subserviently rubbed his stomach.

"What a hussy he is," Liz said, re-entering the room and seeing the pair on the floor. She smiled at the normalcy of it, at the happy everydayness that Casey had brought to Ingrid's life. His unconditional happiness on seeing her, whether she'd been away for hours, or out of the room for mere seconds.

Ingrid raised herself back into her chair and continued to rub the dog's stomach with her foot.

"So how was your day?" Liz asked Ingrid. "Even though you're positively ancient compared to your classmates."

"Not only that," Ingrid began. "They, they are all huge. Taller than me. I... I don't even have, have a height advantage!"

"You're five seven, I wouldn't have called that short."

"Well, it is now. They, they tower over me and they're all kind of... Solid. I feel minute. Timid and minute."

"Timid?"

"Yeah, I... I am a mouse. They are tigers."

"Just pre-semester nerves. You'll be right once you settle down to actually learning things. Do you need assertiveness training, my little mouse, do you think?"

"What is assert... "

"Assertiveness. It's kind of like being self-assured, able to stand up for yourself without being hostile."

"I don't know, those hostile ones seem to get their own way a lot."

"They do, don't they? But it's kind of a hollow victory. You're not so tall if you're just standing on people to gain height."

"I'd rather stay five foot seven."

"That's the way. You'll be okay. But you do need to learn to stand up for yourself a little."

"Why? Can't I just go... go quietly on?"

"I suppose so. But you have to be very wary of people who take advantage of quietness."

"Yes, yes," Ingrid said. "Some people are... mean."

"They are at that."

"What about your day?" Ingrid asked. "You seemed a bit... A bit funny, when I got home. And you have a headache."

Liz did seem sombre. She was slumped a little in her chair, like someone spent, downcast, leaning over her coffee and resting on her elbow. Her usual spark, imperceptible.

"I'm okay, I just... Probably need to get a new job, now that you're managing pretty well. I need to give my brain something to do. Stop it dwelling. Oh, there's my phone again. I'll get it."

'Again?' thought Ingrid, as her mother left the room. She heard Liz answer lightly enough and then the words sank into a solemn murmur before disappearing all together. Liz had taken the phone into her bedroom as she sometimes did when she was talking to her friend, Anne.

Finishing her coffee, Ingrid decided to go into the yard and play with Casey for a while. If Anne was on the phone her mother could be an hour or more. Casey happily chased a ball to the end of the yard but left it there where it stopped and ran back to Ingrid, expectant.

"No," said Ingrid. "I don't think you, you've quite got the, the concept of 'fetch'."

She walked to the fence and retrieved the ball. Casey following delighted.

"He's got you well trained," Liz called from the doorway.

"That was quick," Ingrid called back, throwing the ball towards Liz, Casey chasing. "I thought it was Anne."

"No, not this time. It was Robert."

Liz picked up the ball and threw it; Casey bounded straight after it but kept running after the ball had stopped.

"Silly dog. Policeman Robert?"

"Yep."

"Is he, he coming up?"

"Maybe. Listen, come here a sec, there's some stuff I need to tell you."

Liz took a seat at the outdoor table and waited for Ingrid to join her. The afternoon sun had dropped lower and was squinting through the surrounding treetops before it would dip behind the western hills to make night. The nights were cooling now, summer nearly gone, underscoring the passing of time. Liz felt age weary but shrugged it off as Ingrid slid onto the bench seat opposite.

"Jon Ingram's trial begins at the end of next month," she said without preamble. "The prosecution aren't going ahead with the kidnap and sexual assault charges because he didn't confess during interview, only in unrecorded talk with a detective and now he's denying any involvement and refusing to sign a statement."

"Oh."

"The only way they'll go ahead is if you'll lay charges and testify."

"What does that mean?"

"If you'll file a complaint, make a statement and go to the court and tell them what he did."

"In front of everyone?"

"Yes."

"I... I thought Robert said, said I wouldn't have to."

"He wasn't expecting this retraction. Ingram now denies any involvement in the kidnap. He insists he very often protected you."

"Oh."

Ingrid felt herself go shaky inside. The mouse within searched for somewhere to hide, skittish, out in the wide open and vulnerable. There were the memories so putridly close they could be smelled. *I am safe*, she thought but didn't feel.

"Ingrid?"

"He did... Sometimes. Protect me."

"He now claims he didn't know you were being held against your will."

"Chains weren't a clue?"

"He says he only had consensual intercourse with you, once you were of age."

"Consensual?"

"It means you agreed to have sex with him."

"I... I... No."

"Hon, it's okay."

"No. I was never... Of age. I had no birthdays. I... I did not grow. I was... Was always nine. Nine and scared. Always."

"Well, he faces a long gaol sentence on drugs manufacturing charges, he's doing what he can to make sure nothing is added to it. Making the other matters your word against his."

"I... What am I suppose... I... They... Shit."

"You don't have to do anything today. I just had to tell you where they're at, prosecution-wise. I'm sorry. We thought it would be open and shut."

The mouse stirred again inside Ingrid, that old helplessness. She remembered under the bed, minutes of safety, worth the punishment, but always futile. Small against the wall, skirting trouble, until he dragged her by the chain, harshly to the light.

"They were daddy's friends. They... He did... protect me sometimes. I... I'm... "

"I know, I'd had them in our home a few times. I knew they were mixed up in some petty stuff with your dad, but I never would have expected... I could kill them with my bare hands. I'm so sorry."

"It's not your fault!"

"I should never have let them in our house. How were you supposed to know not to trust them?"

"You've had a bad day with this."

Liz nodded. The unbearable heaviness of guilt.

"They... they are the guilty ones." Ingrid said, guessing precisely Liz's unrest. "Not you."

"I let them in even though I never really trusted that man."

"Only because of my father."

"I still... Never mind. We have some time to work through all this. Are you doing all right?"

"The mouse is safe. Why... why don't we take Casey down... down to the water? Clear our heads."

"Sounds like a plan."

27

Chapter 27

The fall was flawless - it was the landing that would kill her. The fall was free, almost flight, but the end was so obviously near. The sudden descent had started far a way from land. From high, she could see the area, given prevailing wind conditions, where she was going to crash. There was no possible survival. She braced herself and before she knew it, she was on the floor broken and he was standing above her, smiling, drunk.

"Jon's gone. It's my turn."

Oblivious to her pain, her fall, he turned her over roughly. Onto her stomach, face to the ground, and he dragged her underwear pulling to her knees. His entry burned and she cried out. She was already broken, why did he have to keep breaking?

"Oh fuck, that's good," he whispered, his whiskey breath close to her down turned face. "Tight."

She whimpered and the sound woke her, struggling in a wrap of sheets and sweat, heart pounding, the fear and loathing still awake in her.

"Argh!" she said, trying to free herself from it all.

"You all right, hon?" her mother called from the dark.

"I... I need light," Ingrid yowled hoarse, struggling still with the fear and the restrictive tangle of sheets.

The bedroom door opened and the hall light rushed in and rescued Ingrid, her mother quickly too, at her side. Followed by an excited Casey.

"You're soaking," Liz noted, turning on the bedside lamp. "Let's change this bedding. You swap out of your pyjamas while I fetch some fresh sheets."

"I'm sorry," said Ingrid, helping her mother to drag off the wet bedclothes.

"What on earth for?"

"You go... go to sleep never knowing what... what might wake you."

"So do you. Besides, I'd much rather this than waking up not knowing where you are. I'll be back in a minute."

Liz hurried out to bring fresh sheets, chased by Casey, who was enjoying immensely the late-night activity. Ingrid found clean pyjamas. She needed quickly to change into them, as a gossamered shame lay over her body even now, left behind by the dream, unbroken. She did not want her mother to see her degraded self. Her ankle, never quite mended, ached with a very old familiar pain. Without the manacle tight it still felt a burning constriction. A constrict too within the part of Ingrid that wanted to cry out. Too yell, look what you've done to me! To cry, please somebody release me! But it was held in, a long time lost, the way out.

"I am safe," Ingrid whispered to herself, but felt it false. The damage had been done. Something irrevocable, peace. He would be forever carried within her. He had branded her interior, his. Seared his mark on her, in her.

"Is your ankle sore?" Liz asked, returning with new linen.

Ingrid stopped rubbing it and stood to help her mother remake the bed.

"I... No, not so much. I..."

"Do you need pain relief?"

"No. I just... am defeated."

"No, you're not. Well, okay." Ingrid did look despondent, beaten. "Maybe just this round." Liz continued. "But you'll come good. Is this you stressing about Ingram? Look, even if you don't press charges, he's still going to gaol for a very long time, you know, for the drug manufacturing and supplying and those other charges that I can't remember. Pass me a pillowslip. Ta. But hon, for you, there's no fat lady singing, not even a tone-deaf weight watcher nearby. It's not nearly over; you still have life ahead. Hon, listen, I know I've said this ad infinitum, ad nauseam and add any other Latin, but this too will pass."

"Like a kidney stone." Ingrid finished for her.

"That's right. With much pain and swearing but eventual relief. Or at least to a point where you can live contented in your life. I have faith in you."

"Why?"

"Because you're here. You're still here."

"Am I?"

"Yes... You know when I first heard Ingram had retracted his statement, I wanted to go down there and kill him with my bare hands. But he isn't the one, is he?"

The two woman sat on the newly made bed. Ingrid absently rubbing her ankle again. The nightmare's lasting torments seemed to have bundled themselves into a tight spiky mass and drilled down to arrive painfully somatic in her foot.

Liz continued, "He didn't do all the damage to you. The man I want to kill is already dead, and really, I'm not sure I can forgive God for not giving me the chance to kill him outright, myself."

"He's not dead."

"Sorry? Hon, I know nobody could identify the body, but they're pretty sure it's him. Do you still think you've seen him?"

"No. But in here." Ingrid tapped her head and then her heart. "He's still... still inside me, laughing and... "

"Don't let him win, hon. Is your ankle really hurting? You're rubbing it. Need something for it?"

"That batch of ice is ready to go Sydney. I'll drop it on my way through."

"Thanks, Jon. Give a coupla tabs to the kid, she could do with some livening up."

"Are you sure, mate? After what happened with that E. You don't want that crap again. That was full on."

"It was just a bad batch. Give her some. Call it a test."

"Hon?"

"He's always... No. No. My ankle's fine. You... You go back to bed."

"You sure? Where's your wet PJs? I'll throw them in the laundry. Come on Casey, bed."

"He can stay."

"Okay. See you in the morning." Liz hesitated at the door. "You're okay?"

Ingrid smiled a bright reassurance she wasn't sure she felt and Liz left the room. The door remained open wide enough for Casey to move through if he needed to roam. For now he was sound asleep on the bed, legs quivering, chasing dreams.

It was three AM, by the clock and Ingrid felt wide-awake or wide afraid. Afraid of dreams. She slipped into bed, careful, not to disturb the dog or the fresh feeling of clean, brought by the new sheets. Ingrid was intimidated to uncomfortable by the remnant of fear still held in her being and balked at switching off the lamp. The dark, a prison, easy for murky thoughts to gather and dwell. To stay near but hidden until they amassed the strength for an assault and attacked viciously from the black. Ingrid could almost feel them mustering in the background.

To be rid of him, I have to be rid of me. No. Sleep. Sleep is good. There'll be strength in the morning. Death will end it all. Kill him. No. Yes. No.

But the idea of death can ease the intensity of suffering. An out, that can be put safely in a pocket for emergencies, for when it's too much. It never has to be utilised, but knowing it's there... Death can be held over the pain. See, there is a way out. You can hurt me no more.

"Fuck you," Ingrid whispered to his ghost, and she switched off the bedside lamp with resolve, curling around the sleeping dog.

Thoughts, memories, carouselled through but she wouldn't let them slow going past. Wouldn't let them stop and solidify into something coherent and real. Finally, sleep took hold and slipped her away.

The fall was flawless - it was the landing that would kill her.

28

Chapter 28

When morning brought reprieve from dark memories, Ingrid tiredly welcomed the early dazzle and the comfort of it's dawning. The night had been long, time giving the most awful of thoughts length to dwell in. Time to dig into her, engrave a mark, leave her injured more. The remains, she wore like a heavy cloak, difficult to shrug off as she set toward morning routine.

Her mother was busy in the kitchen. There would be coffee and the smell of bread becoming toast. All domestically familiar as it could be, but Ingrid was finding it hard to be usual. She just wanted to say, 'no, too hard,' but that would gain her nothing, plus her mother's scrutiny and perhaps unanswerable questions. Sometimes, merely staying in bed and hiding for a while, just not having to explain would simplify the whole recovery thing. Today is too hard; we'll try again tomorrow. Let's not speak of it all. Let's just be.

"Morning," said Liz, as Ingrid moved her night-time funk into the kitchen. "You okay, after last night?"

"Yeah," Ingrid half lied, knowing the leftover unease should or would eventually dissipate as the day slogged on. "Fine."

"Good. What time's your first class?"

"Not till eleven."

"Good-o. Toast?"

"Hmm."

Humdrums played in the background as Liz busied her self at the kitchen bench, throwing together sandwiches for Ingrid's mid-class lunch break. Morning radio was being enthusiastic, as was Casey, bouncing about looking for the slightest crumb from either Liz or Ingrid. Ingrid relented and gave him the corner of her toast. He gulped it down like the starving and moved to try Liz.

"No you don't, fats. Your circumference is starting to equal your length. You need more exercise," she told the dog.

"I'll take him now, before school. A good walk," Ingrid said.

That word was enough, Casey on hearing of the walk, began sliding around on the tiled floor like a fanatical whirling dervish. Running in small excitement propelled circles. Ingrid poured coffee into a portable lidded coffee mug and the pair headed out into the crunchy leafed cold of the sunny autumn morning. Casey dragged Ingrid to the corner then his pace slowed down to rapid, smelling every plant, bus stop, pole, fence, bush, and tree.

"Let's just walk," Ingrid proposed tugging hard on the leash to rein in the pup and Casey did slow to a human carrying hot coffee trot. They meandered, Ingrid following the dog's zigs and zags until they were down to the seawall near the marina.

The day was beaming pleasant, the water shimmering a reflection of yachts and other maritime postcard shapes. It was difficult to maintain the funk with this backdrop. But Ingrid managed.

She hated such contradiction of mood. Such division. This should be usual; woman takes dog for a walk. No headlines, just normalcy. But Ingrid had so much trouble conducting usual. It constantly ended badly, came undone and left her rented and eventually wary of calm. While she and her mother had worked so hard in creating a stable ordinary, Ingrid hadn't reckoned on his pervasive presence in their everydayness and now Jon Ingram was devalidating what she had been through. Taking away the truth that had been her bloody awful life. There was no man to stand up and say, 'I saw what he did to her.' Ingram had now left her as the nothing his friend had made her. The dehumanised mass he'd sculpted blow by blow.

Sometimes, admittedly on bad days, Ingrid wished she'd never been rescued. Now she had seen how people went about their days.

She saw them buy goods at the shops; she saw them unafraid. They went off to their jobs while she could barely manage a few hours a day at the adult learning centre. She sometimes wet the bed, she woke up afraid, she was awkward around people and if she hadn't been rescued she wouldn't have known any better. Now, every time she woke up racked by memories, haunted by him, she felt she had failed. Failed at letting the past remain where it belonged. Failed at the everydayness.

Ingrid's ankle pained her so she sat on a bench for a while, sipping her coffee, with Casey straining unhappily at the end of the leash. There were seagulls and he felt it his duty to chase them off. But there were no other people about so Ingrid let the dog free and he pelted after the gulls until there were none.

"Well done," Ingrid told him. "The world... world is safe once more."

Ingrid couldn't help but smile at her manic puppy ridding the sea front of the scavenger birds. So seriously he took his mission that he wouldn't let the birds contemplate landing, chasing them if they flew low, aborting their landings.

"Come on, Case. We'd better get back."

The dog returned and Ingrid hooked his leash back on. The waterside was becoming peopled, and Ingrid did not feel like the polite 'good mornings' of the early walker's club, so she headed Casey toward home.

Liz was out in the yard, hanging out washing, when they arrived home. The sheets from the night before, flapping on the line, a reminder of the nightmare. An ensign of failure, it seemed to Ingrid.

"You look a bit woebegone," Liz observed.

"I just... I'm... I can't."

"Is this still the Ingram thing? Put it aside for a while. Talk to Doctor Stedman this arvo. She might see it from a different angle and make things clearer for you."

"It's not... I... I want to be tougher. But all I really want to do is hide."

"Fair enough. But this might change when you've had time to work it out for yourself. If you're not driven to charge Ingram that doesn't mean you're weak. More that you want the past over with and nobody can blame you for that. Okay?"

"Okay. It's just... I."

"I know, it sucks."

"Would you like... Like another coffee?"

"You bet your sweet bippy, I do."

"What's a bippy?"

"I have no idea. Apparently it's sweet. It sounds like a shellfish."

Ingrid moved indoors to brew another coffee, followed by Casey, who flopped into his basket, exhausted after his morning of bird watching and bird chasing. Liz arrived in just as Ingrid poured.

"Perfect timing," she said, sitting at the table. "I'm coming to town later; do you want to meet at Doctor Stedman's and have an early dinner at the pub? It's Tuesday, so it shouldn't be too crowded for you."

"Oh. Okay."

"Don't be frightened. It's just dinner, and maybe some wine. If it gets too much, we'll just leave."

"Okay."

When Ingrid reached Doctor Stedman's the afternoon sun was already low and an autumn cool was taking hold again. Ingrid wished she'd brought a jacket, she hated to be cold. In the waiting room, she shook a little.

"Ingrid, would you like to come in?" Doctor Stedman asked.

Ingrid was never quite sure if she was supposed answer. If she were honest, perhaps not today, doctor. I'll just sit here for a while and then go home. But Ingrid rose and followed the doctor into her office.

"How's your week been?" the doctor asked when they'd settled into their chairs.

Ingrid struggled to tell her about Jon Ingram and how she felt he'd betrayed her yet again by the retracting of his statement.

"Are you going to pursue it?"

"I... No. Do you think that... That's cowardly?"

"Do you?"

"Yes."

"It's not so much cowardice, but self-protection. You are, I imagine, frightened of the process. Frightened by what might happen in the court room."

"I... I'm..."

"Go on."

"I'm frightened too, that I... I will feel... Sorry for him."

"Hmm. Have you ever heard of coercion? The less informed would call it Stockholm Syndrome."

29

Chapter 29

Outside was blue and crisp. Summer had really left without evident trace and only a few people persisted with short sleeves in the autumn brisk. Ingrid huddled in a long tee and jacket, sure that her internal thermostat was out of order. Inside, the warmed-up librarians appeared industrious, making their final preparations before opening the doors. A little covey of nannies and poppies accumulated on the doorstep, bags bulging with books to be returned and Ingrid was not uncomfortable on the fringe listening to them greet happily and comment on the weather. There was also much timepiece comparison as opening time drew closer.

"I have two minutes to."

Ingrid stole a look at her own watch and thought perhaps it slow against the nanny poppy aggregate. As the group began to murmur mutinously, with much tisking, the doors were opened, averting a grey quiet riot by mere seconds. Ingrid stood away and let the clatter of elderly rush slowly to the book return shoot and empty their bags before entering the library proper.

It was in the biography section that Ingrid noted a dank smell.

Hard against the floor, the smell of old water in the rotting carpet. He brandished his already opened penknife, always lovingly sharpened to a dangerous gleam, and the threat was very real on his face.

"Don't move, bitch!"

But he moved roughly, to face her feet, on his knees straddling her heavily, and inserted the knife inside. Inside where she was already sore. His angry thrusting.

"If you struggle I'll cut your fucking cunt to shreds! Now suck me off."

When he thrust his penis into her face, in reflex she pulled away and immediately felt the knife burn.

"Young lady? Are you all right?"

Ingrid could only run. Direction irrelevant, just away.

30

Chapter 30

In another room someone was crying. Sad, mourn filled, more than simple tears. Well beneath a wail, catching, muted perhaps in deference to the night. Others slept, medicated dreams, gaining strength to do battle in the next morn. Fighting was their lives. Waking hours were consumed by ugly brutal immortal combat. War fatigue had long ago taken dogged grip, but they fought on, tired, valiant against their invisible enemies.

Ingrid lay awake plagued still by her interior adversaries. One of them, a type of inglorious, earned, conditional, but dubious, surrender. Give up? Yes. How simple would it be? To go basic. Primary needs only. To eat mind-numbing medications and care only about the when, where and what of the next meal and agree in essence that this was as good as it was ever going to get. No casualties. No real expectations. Her mother could rest easy. Ingrid could live a long, quiet life and die eventually of undiagnosed boredom and the long-term effects of medications for the sake of peace. Simple.

Her mother could rest easy.

"Can't you sleep, Ingrid?" The night nurse asked on the next round. "The doctor has you charted for a sleeping tablet, would you like it?"

Simple.

***

The autumn had turn wet, grey, the hues all wrong for the season. Day after day, dull, dismal, everything the colour of an old paling fence. Ingrid had cabin fever, but she would've had that confined in the hospital whatever the weather.

"I've left a soggy umbrella in every bus in town," Liz complained, shaking off the damp. "Where do they all go, I ask you? There must be truckloads of lost brolleys somewhere. Perhaps that's the apocalypse. When the four horsemen appear the unbelievers will be beaten to death by all the umbrellas they have ever lost."

"Sounds... Sounds feasible."

"And hula-hoops."

Ingrid smiled; Liz was having a rant in a psych ward.

"I have never... Lost an umbrella..."

"Hmm. Not sure with what you'll be smited. You probably won't be smit, smote, whatever, at all. You are unbelievably careful with your stuff."

"I lost that school... School cardigan... In... In kindergarten."

"Do you remember that? Well, that's it then, you'll be slapped repeatedly with a school cardy when the end is nigh. Where's a nurse? Let's see if you can go out for a real coffee."

"Yes. Yes."

Under Liz's latest umbrella they huddled up to the hospital's cafe, grateful to reach it's dry warmth and aroma. A place on the grounds where the smell of hospital grade bleach hadn't permeated through all nooks. It was too crowded for Ingrid but she held tough, for it was still preferable to the ward. The noise, the people - but coffee. They found seats and Liz went to the queue, to order and collect the brews.

"Here we go. Two coffees to stay."

The first sip was heavenly and then it just became coffee, but Ingrid had no real desire to become a coffee snob, she was off that ward, it could taste like camel sweat for all she cared.

"When can I come home?" she asked Liz.

"I don't know. You know what the doctors are like, they'll have to tweak your medication some, to feel they're doing something. Dr Stedman will probably have a chat with you and you never know you might be out by the end of the week. How's your hand? You punched that wall pretty hard, apparently."

Ingrid shrugged. "End of the weak," she mumbled.

"Sorry?"

"It's okay. My hand is okay."

"Good. Don't do that again, okay? You've been hurt enough already. I nearly had a coronary when the police car pulled up. Her, next door enjoyed it immensely."

"That's why I had, had an... An 'episode.' For her next door."

The woman next door neighbour had become Liz's nemesis after she complained about where Liz put the bins out on garbage night.

"Well, she rushed straight across the road to Mrs Whatsit's, so they could watch together. Hoping for a spectacle."

"Did you give them one?"

"No. Unfortunately I could think of nothing to do but wave meekly."

"Sad."

"Next time I'll try to remember to burst into song when emergency vehicles arrive at the door."

"There won't be, be a next time," Ingrid said. "I can't do this again." There was melancholy.

"Hon, if it happens again, it happens again and we deal with it."

"I'm so tired."

"I know, I know. But look how far you've come. Of course you're tired! You've had a monster growth spurt. Adolescence, schooling, living skills, dog training; you pack more into a month than most people do in a decade."

"You're just saying that."

"I know, but I'm meaning it too. Can you cope with another coffee? I just see you on that ward reduced to decaf, it tears at a mother's heart strings."

Ingrid smiled and Liz jumped up with her purse to buy them fresh coffees. She was soon back and clattered the mugs on to the table.

"Sorry," she said, wiping up the spills with a paper napkin. "This is why my career as a waitress was cut very short."

"You were a waitress?"

"For ten minutes in the seventies. I was fired for my absolutely incredible incompetence. Funny now."

"Can't... Can't see you as in... Incompetent."

"Oh, I was so awful, I was brilliant. Now, of course, I could do it standing on my head, but back then... Anyway, just goes to show how far people can come. These days after I burn a meal I can at least get it to the table without injury to any of my diners. You too, could develop talents like mine. Hit or miss cooking notwithstanding. Speaking of food, do you want something here? Your nurse said you've not been eating properly."

To erase him, she had to erase herself.

"No, thanks. Coffee is good."

"You should eat, or they'll make you stay in longer."

"Oh. Okay. Maybe. Maybe a cake."

"That's the way. I'll bring you back something nice."

Liz was off again. *Too much coffee,* Ingrid thought.

The noise in the cafe seemed to ebb and swell in sudden strident sound waves that almost took Ingrid under, while she waited for her mother. She floundered some but fought and kept her head above and sipped her coffee with the slight quake of the fragile.

"Mud cake," Liz announced, setting down with a clink and a rattle; two plates, forks and fresh napkins. "Get stuck in."

"Stuck in mud, yes."

Liz smiled at the sign of humour.

"I've been thinking," she said. "Next semester break we should do something holiday-like. Find a dog friendly caravan park, hire one those caravan wagon things and have a change. What do you think? We have fifteen years of holidays to catch up on. Go north to warmer climes."

"I like the idea of warmer."

"Okay. I'll look into it. Surf the net, be a travel agent brochure poacher. Maybe you could take some driving lessons in the meantime."

Ingrid coughed, groped for air and Liz smacked her on the small of the back until the cake crumbs dislodged and Ingrid could intake air again comfortably.

"Sorry!" Liz said. "I didn't mean to startle you."

Ingrid's eyes still watered, "I'm okay," she said. "Did you... I... I can't even push the lawn mower in a... In a straight line. I'm not sure."

"Relax. It's a rite of passage, and driving is a handy skill. You'll be fine. I'll be the one in panic. I nearly drove my poor mother to a nervous breakdown, and definitely the drink. It's only fair that you too have this same curious opportunity. Call it a family tradition."

"I never gave... Gave it any thought."

"You'll get used to the idea. Anne's letting us have her son's car, he's backpacking 'round Europe for three months or so."

"Backpacking?"

"Travelling. You know, with all his clothes and gear in a packpack. Another rite of passage, really. Maybe you'll do it one day."

"I..."

"It's not obligatory. I don't think I can finish this cake. Phew, I'm stuffed."

"Me either."

"You sure? Promise me you'll eat while you're in here. You look like you've dropped under fifty kilos again. You know, you'll be out soon and back to my sometimes-successful cooking. Which reminds me I must replace the batteries in the fire alarms. So feast while you can, okay? Take seconds, thirds."

"Okay."

"Promise?"

"Okay."

"Well, I guess we should get you back."

"Oh."

"I'll stay for a bit, then I'm taking the train to Anne's to pick up the car. So I'll be able to take you home on leave for a bit tomorrow. How's that sound?"

They rose leaving their debris and headed for the door.

"Sounds very good," Ingrid answered.

They crossed the road and as they neared the doors to the unit Ingrid became hesitant.

"It's okay, hon. It won't be for much longer."

Liz buzzed the intercom and spoke.

"Pox!" she said as they waited for a nurse to let them in. "I forgot my new umbrella! It's up at the cafe."

31

Chapter 31

When Ingrid was discharged from the psychiatric unit she was stilled somewhat of her dis-ease but within days a vague unhappiness suggested itself in the somatic guise of a bone deep weariness. Lethargic, she lay on her bed with Casey. He asleep snoring slightly, she, not quite thinking. There was blue sky inviting outside but Ingrid lay there, still.

Liz had taken the borrowed car to the carwash to thoroughly clean it inside and out, to rid it of 'the teenage boy mank,' she said.

Dishes lay strewn about the kitchen sink; Ingrid on a promise to have them done by the time Liz returned. Finally moved off the bed by a sense of housework burden, Ingrid dawdled into the kitchen.

"Shit," she mumbled on seeing the breakfast debris.

The pile from Ingrid's fatigued point of view, looked insurmountable.

"Bollocks," she said. "Why'd we have bacon and eggs?"

It was a push. Feeling like she'd rather lie under the kitchen table in the foetal position, Ingrid filled the sink with hot water and suds and began by dropping in the congealed egg covered plates.

There was a frantic scratching at the back door. With this persuasion Ingrid left her chore to let the dog outside. Casey bounded down into the yard. With a quick convincing argument in ergonomics, Ingrid decided to drop on to the sun soaked back step and wait for the dog rather than return to her task only to be called back to let him in.

Ingrid allowed her mind to wander off completely and sat blankly enjoying the sun on her face. In this almost nothingness, she didn't hear Liz return from the car wash and was startled with a heart pounded chest, off the step and nearly into a run when Liz spoke.

"I'm so sorry," Liz then said. "I thought you'd heard me come in."

"I'm, I'm okay," Ingrid assured, clutching her chest in contradiction.

"I should have those slippers with bells on, like you had when you were a toddler, so I could always hear where you were, then you might have heard me coming."

"I'm... I'm usually more, um, on guard."

"Yes, you are. Maybe that's a good sign. You feel safe enough here to drop your guard."

"Maybe."

With the extra adrenaline the shock had brought, Ingrid felt able to tackle the dishes. She went in doors, with Liz and Casey following in a confusion of legs.

"I thought you'd be done with those," Liz said.

"I... I was letting them... Ah, soak."

"Right." Liz was a tad sceptical. "Sounds like me waiting for the weeds in the garden to grow long enough to get a good grip on."

"Yeah."

"You do seem a little lethargic. Is it the medications?"

"I hope so. I wouldn't like to think this was just me."

"Mention it to Doctor Stedman tomorrow."

"I will if I can be bothered."

"Is that you joking?"

"Sort of."

* * *

"I... I think that I am unhappy." Ingrid told the doctor near the end of her session the next day.

"What makes you say that?"

"I... I don't know. It's not right... To feel... Feel like this."

"Feel how?"

"I... It's hard to do anything."

"How do you mean?"

"I can... barely be bothered to tell you. I... I can't get in the... Shower, and when I finally do, I can't get out. Water restrictions."

"Hmm. Go on."

Ingrid shrugged. "I don't know. Everything's... Everything's a supreme effort. Falling behind at school. Don't want to get... out... Out of bed. It's all wrong. I... I have no right, and I have no right... to..."

"Do you think I should up your venlafaxine?"

"Maybe."

"Why do you feel you have no right?"

"Everything is good. The best it's ever... Been... And I shouldn't be so... down. I should... Should be exceedingly happy."

"Not all depression is reactionary."

"Then, it's not fair."

"Yes. Depression's not fair. It's an outrageous enemy. But, you have to fight."

"Why? Fuck. I'm tired."

"I know. Look, we'll up the venlafaxine. Give it a few weeks and if you still feel this way, we'll rethink."

"You won't lock... Lock me up, will you?"

"No. No. Hospital's the last resort."

"It's no resort."

The doctor smiled. "No, it's definitely not that sort of resort," she said. "It's a latter alternative, if it gets too bad for you."

"And there's... "

"There's what?"

"Something... I... There's... Behind me. I don't know. There's a... Something coming."

"A flashback?"

"I don't know. Maybe."

There occurred a small silence between the women. Comfortable but then not.

"It's... " began Ingrid, filling in the widening gap.

"It's?"

"It's like when... I was locked in the... The cupboard. Frightened of the dark... But... Shit."

"Go on."

Ingrid moved uncomfortable in her seat. Uncomfortable in her skin. Uncomfortable in her head.

"I don't want to... Remember."

She looked around the room, so familiar now. Bookshelf, filled with psychology related words. Desk, topped with scattered lives, manila folders seeping pages of people's troubled biographies.

"Remembering is not where the pain lies. The pain is in you. Remembering helps get it out."

"When? Just when am I going to be all right?"

The doctor didn't answer, perhaps she couldn't. "In the cupboard," she said instead. "You were frightened, but?"

"I don't know," Ingrid gave a shrug, not through indifference, but lack of the words. "I... There was a vicious peace... In there."

"Vicious?"

"I don't know if that's the... The right word. I... In there, while the door was locked I was... Untouched. But every heard footsteps, my... my heart would leap in the dark." Ingrid felt her heart do exactly that now. "Jesus."

"It's okay," the doctor said. "You're okay. Keep going. I'm here, beside you."

"When the door opened."

"Come here, you! Hope you've fuckin' learnt your lesson."

He pulled her out by the arm and smashed her naked self against the wall. He dragged her roughly along it toward the upturned wooden crate.

"Get on it!"

"No," she said, but stepped onto the crate facing the wall.

Now at the right height, he pushed her onto the wall and entered from behind. Ripping immediately. Blood ran.

"Fuck you!" he whispered hostile. "Fuck you!" again.

It was only his weight sandwiching her to the wall that kept her upright. She would crumble when he was spent.

"Ingrid? How old were you? Ingrid?" The doctor called from the present.

"I was nine." Ingrid answered when she was almost back. "Always nine. Until they found me... I was forever nine. Not... Not very tall."

"He was a monster."

A moment can freeze you in grim reality time before releasing you, less innocent, never quite the same. The residue of the flashback sat heavy upon Ingrid. She felt a longing to cry. Her backside pained where he had left his mark and she moved now uncomfortable on the soft chair. A longing to cry.

"Are you okay?" The doctor asked, then answered herself. "No, you're not. Don't leave just yet. Have a hot drink, if you like. Coffee? Sit for a while."

32

Chapter 32

Sometimes Ingrid was not sure how she stumbled her way home after a session with Doctor Stedman. She couldn't quiet remember 'good-byes', leaving the office, walking to the bus stop. The bus ride home, a blank black space where movement should've been. A travel card in her hand, undeniable proof of a journey taken. Yet, there was Casey bounding about in the backyard. Ingrid was home.

Time travel was draining. Past and nowness sometimes crashed together like poorly played cymbals, untriumphant and discordant. Leaving Ingrid crumpled, wondering where she was. She sat down on the back steps, easing herself into the now. Taking in the sounds of her mother moving busy about inside. Hearing birds squawk and trill. Casey barked. Now was quite loud.

"Cup of tea?" Liz called from the kitchen.

"Yes, please," Ingrid answered, rising from the step. "It's getting pretty cold out," she said as she moved inside.

"Winter's just about here."

Time moved them forward and Ingrid felt the machination. She felt a little caught. Where was she going? If she were to stand still just for a moment would she see her place?

"You look thoughtful," Liz observed. "Let's go and flop on the lounge. Catch up."

Tea safely on the coffee table, which seemed wrong, the two sprawled, plumping cushions and nestling in.

"So," began Liz. "What's going on with you?"

"I have no purpose."

"Jeez, I thought you'd tell me about overdue library books or what assignments you have to do. Way to start heavy."

"I'm sorry."

"No. No. I'm only stirring you. I'm sorry. What brought this on?"

Casey hurtled in and jumped up to flop in-between them on the couch. Ingrid scratched him absently on the head, as he settled into sleep.

"I... I kind of... Just time keeps going present and past and passed... And one day it'll all be over... And why was I? What am I supposed to be doing? The... The first part of my... my life was such... a waste... I don't want to waste the next..."

"You're not the first to ask *what am I doing here?* It happens to everybody, more or less."

"But... Sometimes, sometimes you have to have a reason for being."

"Mine is to eat chocolate cake."

"What? I... "

"I didn't mean to be glib. Sorry. Some people go their entire lives just existing. Scratching to stay alive. We kind of have the luxury to question. A luxury you once didn't have. But now that you do, it's not surprising that it's utterly confusing. You've come in early for your mid-life crisis."

"I... I don't know how I turned, turned this... this latest what? Ordinary, ordinary household depression into a crisis. Is this a crisis?"

"I don't know. I'm no philosopher, but choosing your road can be done lightly or seriously. The end is the same. Nobody comes out alive."

"I want to go lightly but..."

"I know you're under a heavy load. Look, keep questioning but don't let it weigh you down any further."

"I..."

"Nobody really knows."

"Some people seem so... certain."

"Well, if they never have an existentialistic dilemma, good luck to them. I'll just go quietly about my business eating chocolate cake."

Time sat still a little then for Ingrid, sitting on the lounge with her mother and her dog, and lo, it was good. But then the phone rang and it was Robert.

33

Chapter 33

"Fuck, fuck, fuckety, fuck, fuck," Liz murmured pleasantly enough as she returned from taking the telephone call, musical almost. But in contrast, physically she was white and shaky.

"Everything okay?" Ingrid asked, made wary and protective by Liz's uncharacteristic lilting but profane language.

"It was Robert," Liz answered.

"Okay?" Ingrid asked again.

"Jon Ingram is getting reduced charges in return for information on the Scandinavian drug syndicate he was involved in. Misdemeanour."

"What does that mean?"

"He could be out in six months."

"Out?"

"Yep. With time served since his arrest he could be out by early next year."

"They've... They've just not worried about me?"

Tears slid down Liz's face.

"They've bigger fish to fry," she said, hurt. "Apparently."

"Oh."

***

Ingrid wasn't sure how she felt about being put aside for the greater good, so easily forgotten. She'd spent a long time forgotten. This fresh disregard brought her memory unsteadily back to the long nights secured to the tree, out alone by the creek, and not even, Gyro, the dog, as tethered company. Afraid and unafraid. Afraid for what would be, unafraid in the short space of safeness she had. Untouched minutes. Now, she'd allowed Ingram original immunity, by letting the police concentrate on the drug charges. She had. They'd assured her he'd receive a heavy, prolonged, sentence. That he'd pay in some way for what had happened to her. But nothing. Forgotten. Afraid and unafraid.

Chained to the tree, that tree, she had been eased slightly by the three hundred and sixty degrees of open plain view. If she remained upright alert there could be no vicious surprises. She could see. See anything coming, from any direction. Then the dark would fall all heavy and illusory. Eerie shadows, dark movement and deceptive sound. And she would shrink and ball inside herself, blind panic building. Dark and unseeing, angry with her own warped anticipation she'd want him to come take her finally. Put her out of the waiting sharp misery.

She couldn't quite remember when she lost her future, when she could hold it no longer in her mind. Lost the dreams of what she would be when she grew. It just disappeared, her destiny. It faded out of the realm of her amputated, damaged imagination. She couldn't contemplate any further ahead than her next pee or being towed unwilling back to the house, dog-tired alert and beaten. The persistent rhythm of self-talk, of dreaming the future, beat irregular then halted altogether. They had left her empty.

That Jon Ingram now had a future to happily contemplate unbalanced Ingrid somehow. She teetered. In the unsteady blur, she couldn't see what was to happen. From what direction it would come. He would be out there. Free, laughing.

At least chained to that tree she could fucking see. No future, but she could see the present, the actual. See who was nearby. When they were coming. Fuck!

Where to put this anger?

There were no words. Nothing to spit out. The venom, the anger, was inside, bitter, corrosive.

Fuck!

The anger grew sudden movement. Ingrid jolted, threw herself outside. What made her grab the paring knife from the knife block as she rushed through the kitchen, was reflex. Came from deep and she was unaware.

"Where are you going?" Liz called from the front door. "Your jacket! It's cold! Have you got your phone?"

"Walk!" Ingrid managed, calling from the gate. No stopping. She'd somewhere, or nowhere, to go. Action pulsed the venom furiously further, throughout her taut body. Ingrid sped along the path, perceiving the acrid taste of this anger, caustic on her tongue. 'Fuck!' she spat.

Down, still raging within, at the harbour-side she slowed, breath biting her chest. It was quiet, few people about. Ingrid came upon a tree by the waterside. A tree, safe. A view all around. She would see it coming, whatever it was. The knife was in her hand; she saw and immediately received it. Rubbing a thumb along the steel, Ingrid touched its cold sharpness, acknowledging the bite of the blade. Anger wanted movement still, so she paced around beneath that tree, with no other place for the anger to go but around. At moments she would stop and see the knife in her hand and feel something close.

"Argh!" came a cry from beneath and the intensity of the inner fury twisted her. "Fuck!"

And then it came, a sudden wrathful cut and the blood. Beneath the tree, safe, she hadn't seen it coming. It was so wrong. She was wrong, and her wrongness seeped red for any passer-by to see. Ingrid drooped to the ground vanquished, to sit back leaning weak on the solid tree trunk. Under the naked winter branches, she felt the anger dissipate in brief surrender as her sleeve coloured dark.

"Ingrid?"

She looked up to see Liz, the familiar concern, and was chastened.

"I'm sorry."

"No. No! Don't be. Fuck them all!" Liz said, vehement.

She dropped down next to her child. An arm went protectively around Ingrid's shoulders. Ingrid stiffened but did not pull away.

"I'm sorry," the child, Ingrid, repeated. "I... I cause you grief."

"No, hon. No."

"I do."

"I'd rather cry forever with you, than have never found you again. This is still better."

"I... I... I just want..."

"I know, hon."

"I'm... I'm fucked in the head."

"You're not. But it's still better... It's still better. Let me see your arm... Oh, hon!"

"Please. Let's... Let's not move just yet."

Ingrid wanted the safety of the tree. Wanted to be there under the tree with her mother's arm around her. Contact. It can be so painfully electric, but other times, without shock, it quietened the turmoil.

"Someone should pay," muttered Liz, pulling a handkerchief from her shoulder bag, to press hard against Ingrid's wound.

"I am."

Liz could quell the bleeding but could not still Ingrid's inner disquiet. Could not make it better for her child and this fractured further her sense of parental adequacy.

"I love you," she said simply.

"I know."

That was really all a parent could hope for eventually, wasn't it? That a child knew without doubt that she was loved.

"I have the car just up there. We should get you to the medical centre. I think you need stitches," Liz said.

"Don't let them... Let them. Don't lock me up."

"Let's just get you patched up."

"I'm sorry."

"No, hon. Please don't. You're not the one who should be sorry."

34

Chapter 34

"Robert's coming up on the weekend," Liz told Ingrid.

"Oh. Okay."

"He wants to see you. Explain."

Ingrid placed the Car Driver's Manual she'd been studying open face down on her lap.

"There's nothing to explain," she said.

"Well, he thinks there is."

"Well, maybe he can explain roundabouts," Ingrid said tapping the manual on her lap.

"You can use my method," Liz supposed. "When approaching a busy roundabout, close your eyes and enter assertively, hoping for the best."

"Maybe you're not the best person to teach me to drive."

* * *

Ingrid's grin gave much away. Successful. In the coffee shop, she placed the new yellow Learner plates on the table in front of Liz.

"You got them!"

"Yes. Computer test, pass... passed. I am allowed on... on the road with a responsible fully licensed driver, or... or you, as passenger."

"Hey! So, let me buy you a cappuccino. Well done!"

Liz jumped up as Ingrid sat down, a seesaw. Sitting without perfect posture, at last Ingrid could relax after the tense uneasy interaction with both human and computer at the crowded, harried staffed Service NSW Centre. There is a perceivable sigh of satisfaction. A small exhalation drifting out attainment, hard won achievement. Pride-filled bright tick placed in the column marking accomplishments in life. Slightly more balanced now, levered with the failures. Unsteady seesaw life.

"Did you get any questions wrong?" Liz asked, returning with steaming mugs.

"Something... something about closing your eyes when approaching a roundabout. Apparently, you don't."

"Tell me you didn't!"

Ingrid grinned.

"Show me," Liz asked. "Let's see your photo."

"It's horrible."

"They all are. Like passport photos."

Ingrid reluctantly pulled her purse out of her shoulder bag and showed her mother the new license.

"It's not so bad," said Liz. "At least you look human."

"Show me yours."

"I don't think so. Some things are better left unread."

"Go on. I... I showed you mine."

"Okay, but in my defence, I was tired."

"In... in that case, the defence rests. Show me."

"Okay, but I do look like a stunned mullet."

"What's a mullet?"

"A fish."

Liz pushed her purse across the table towards Ingrid, who picked it up to open. Inside, beneath the plastic-coated window sat a photograph of a child, smiling, mischief evident in her eyes, holding an easy open gaze.

"Is that really me?"

"Yep. And quite obviously I didn't pass on the stunned mullet gene. Look at that grin."

Ingrid did look, but it made her disquiet, the she she used to be. The potential stolen, broken and returned invalidate. She pulled her mother's driver's license from it's sleeve, hurriedly, to move away from her once self.

"I... I see what you mean. You look, look..."

"Dazed? It's a mug shot waiting to happen. I hadn't even thought to brush my hair. A failure to pretty womankind everywhere. Ten-year license too. I still have to live with it for another five or so years."

"Could you, you maybe 'lose' it?"

"I could. But the next one might be even worse. Anyway, forget photos, let's drive out to the industrial area and you can have a driving lesson there."

"What? Are you sure? I might kill us."

"Not at the speed you'll be doing. You might slightly maim us."

"I... I don't want to, to slightly maim you."

"I have every confidence in you. There'll be no maiming today."

"I... I... "

"Nerves. Come on, finish your coffee. You'll do fine."

* * *

"The first thing you do is check your review mirror and make sure your make-up's okay. It's important to remember that the paramedics will often work harder to revive you if you're good looking."

"I don't wear... Wear make up."

"I'm just joking. A bit of pre-driving levity. Just check all your mirrors and make sure they're in the right position for you to see. Your side mirrors should..."

Liz went through the basic driver preliminaries with Ingrid. Finally, they were ready to go.

"Now ease out the clutch..."

"Ease... Ease it out of what? Where has it..."

"The pedal on the left. While pressing on the accelerator, let the clutch come up. Like a seesaw. One goes down as the other comes up."

* * *

"Are you all right?"

"I'm just going to pull into this drive-in bottle shop," Liz answered. "That was good for your first ever go."

* * *

Liz arranged for Ingrid to undergo driving lessons with a well insured professional. She also ensured the instructor was female and asked to speak with her before the lesson.

"Don't physically touch her or invade her space," Liz said to the instructor when they met. "Ingrid's speech is hesitant but her mind is very quick. If anything should upset her behaviour just get her back quick."

"Her behaviour?" the instructor asked, looking unsure.

"No, don't worry! It should be fine. Really. I'm sorry if I've given you the wrong impression, she's just had a hard time and deals with stuff a little differently, that's all. She'll be great."

"All right," the instructor said. "Okay, that's cool. I have my mobile. I'll call if anything gets beyond me."

It was Liz's turn to feel unsure. The instructor, the woman, the girl, only looked about twelve years old. How level-headed could she be only ten minutes out of high school?

"I'll get Ingrid," Liz said. "She's just inside."

"Don't... don't watch me leave, please," Ingrid asked as she headed outside, the whiplash inducing kangaroo leaps of her first driving lesson with Liz yet to be repressed.

"Okay. But you'll do fine. See you when you get back."

Ingrid left the house, nervous but determined. Liz heard the vehicle start to an easy chugging and an apparent smooth take-off as the sound faded away down the street. For a moment she felt lost in a mixture of trepidation and pride. Her child taking a drive toward independence. It was how it should be.

35

Chapter 35

Again, how evocative the night. Midnight dark grew remembrances thick and murky, hooking perceptions sharp from unlit recesses and pulling them to the fore shadows. Ingrid hated to know they were there, persistent, pernicious waiting. She could nudge them away, but it was like pushing a fog. Seeping traces yet.

In the distant, a gloomy train call, added soundtrack to Ingrid's rolling disquiet. She turned over in her bed, tried to move her mind to somewhere else. The haunting shouldn't go on. Ingrid felt the sudden, bloody, severed end of her stretched imprisonment should have meant the end of haunting, but it really was only the beginning. Before, reality had been brutal enough, no time or space for preoccupation.

Ghost stories from her faraway childhood had always been set in gloomy haunted landscapes, not happening deep dark inside people. Places were haunted, not people. Ingrid took this her portable haunting within her everywhere and the veracity detonated a small fresh charge of self-anger, at yet another apparent debility. It seemed she possessed such a poor aptitude for leaving the past behind. Dead was supposed to be buried, and for goodness' sake, remain so. She wanted to leave the dark landscape of memory behind. Turn the page. Find the happily ever after.

Would she be this haunted if he hadn't been killed? Had she seen him walked away by the police, handcuffed, caught, beaten but alive, would she be so haunted now? Was it possible the day might come when all her nightmares weren't linked to his psychopathic self?

Sleep came through for a while, drooping over Ingrid heavily like a malaise. It harboured in sombre dreams where Ingrid needed to escape; run for her life, but her legs, suddenly leaden, wouldn't move. She tried dragging herself with her arms as oars, away from the unnamed terror but felt futility take a grip. Ingrid knew his presence near and was about to face the unspeakable when she awoke horrified, drenched.

Casey arrived at her side as Ingrid pulled the damp bedding from her bed and threw each sheet onto a pile with her wet pyjamas. The dog eager to join whatever night sport might be happening bounced a top the sodden pile.

"Hey!" Ingrid hissed. "This isn't a game," she whispered.

But why shouldn't it be? Casey was right, make light, the world was dark enough.

"Come on, let's put this stuff in the washing machine and then go for a walk."

Walk. An enchanted word in Doglish. Casey, eager to begin this new adventure rushed at Ingrid, almost knocking her off balance as she added more layers of warm for the night air.

As ever, putting a leash on the whirling dervish proved a challenge, but finally the pair hit the cold pavement and set a brisk pace toward the dawn. It was freezing. Breath came outdoors shocked to a visible mist by the cold. Ingrid adjusted her scarf over a gap and zipped her jacket higher.

"Mate, you ought'a cover the girl more. She's freezing. At least a pair of socks."

"Fuck off. Why don't you go warm her right up then, stud?"

"Oh... Okay."

"Go on, don't be shy. It's like screwing someone with Parkinson's, mate. Feels good. Shaking in all the right places. Makes a change from her fucking normal imitation dead body shit."

Ingrid shivered, shaking off the disturbance of haunting recollection and stepped up the pace to put distance between past and now.

Casey was almost running but still managed to dart at interesting smells as they passed.

When her breathing eventually laboured, Ingrid slowed to a brisk walk and Casey had time to pee on every other tree. His unsinkable exuberance for life staggered Ingrid. Everything was joyous discovery, exciting and apparently, the whole world his toilet. Ingrid bagged his fresh poop and carried it with caution, until they reached a rubbish bin near the yacht club.

There was nobody about, safe, Ingrid let Casey off the leash and he bounded towards the water.

"Stay local," Ingrid called.

The sun had just begun to squint over the eastern hills, the sky marbled in smears of morning colour. Bright life affirming everydayness. Light began to infiltrate Ingrid's residual dark and she felt tension slip and abate. A suitable stick was found and a lively game of fetch was instigated until Ingrid tired of retrieving it.

"You're su... supposed to get the stick, doof. Come on," she said. "Let's walk some more, then the... the bakery."

* * *

"Croissants," Ingrid said giving the bag to a just sleep emerging Liz.

"Yum," yawned Liz. "Thanks."

"What ti... time is your boyfriend get... Getting here?"

"Don't tease your mother this early in the morning. Besides, he wants to see you. 'Bout eleven. Must have coffee, now. Hurry. Put it on."

"I'm hurrying."

"Faster. Coffee."

"It's on. So's the... the oven. Where's the croissants?"

"I don't know. Where'd I put them?"

"Here they are. On... on the fridge."

"I need coffee."

"Yes... Yes, you do."

"What time's your driving lesson?"

"Eleven, too."

"Eleven to what?"

"I... I meant eleven also, the... the 'as well' too. As when... when Robert gets here."

"Oh. I thought eleven minutes to was a bit precise."

"Here... here drink this coffee, quick."

"So, you'll be home by twelve."

"Probably closer, closer to eleven minutes past."

"Stop teasing, you. Are those croissants hot?"

* * *

"You can reverse park behind that car outside your house."

"I'd rather not, it's my, my mum's friend's car."

"All the better. You need to be able to park under pressure."

"Oh."

"It's okay. You'll be fine."

"What if I hit... Hit it?"

"I'm heavily insured and I have faith in you. Now indicate and pull up beside it. That's the way. Oo, nice car."

"Don't... Don't say that!"

When Ingrid safely finished her lesson and went indoors, Liz and Robert were found out in the backyard firing up the barbecue for lunch. Ingrid heard her mother laugh at something the policeman said and it was nice to hear.

"Ah, the safe return," Liz said, as Ingrid joined them. "How was your lesson?"

"Only... Only five thousand dollars worth of dam... damage this time."

"Well done."

Robert raised an eyebrow in question but remained in bemused silence.

"There's an open wine in the fridge," Liz added.

"Hello," Ingrid said to Robert.

"Hi. How's it going?"

"Not bad."

A slightly protracted silence puffed up between them and Ingrid slipped backward.

"Will... will I bring the bottle?" she asked, retreating. "And a beer?"

"Please," answered Liz. "And I forgot the oil."

"Okay. Casey, race."

Ingrid sprinted to the steps, with Casey giving spirited chase.

"She seems happy," Robert said.

"On the whole, she is," Liz agreed. "But sometimes... "

"Sometimes?"

"Sometimes she struggles with her demons."

"Does she talk about the farm much?"

"Not to me. Maybe with her doctor."

"I wish I could make her pain go away."

"Each good day is a step further away from it, but sometimes something brings it near and it hurts all over again for her."

"She should apply for victim's compensation. I have some pamphlets in the car about it."

"I don't know, she hates the label, 'victim'. It implies ongoing."

"It's for ex-victims of crime too."

"Here she comes."

The dog burst from the house with Ingrid following, juggling oil, wine, a glass and beer. Robert went to help.

"Th... Thanks."

"No problem. You know, I came here to personally apologise for the police Ingram sell-out. It's fucked. Sorry. It just makes me really angry. It was a bloody unforgivable pass over."

"It's not... not your fault."

"I feel like it is. The Police let you down. In a really big way."

"Come on, you two. What's a person gotta do for oil 'round here?" Liz called from the barbecue. "I'm starving."

"I am really sorry," repeated Robert, earnest.

"I'll live."

"I know you will. You're doing so well. But, if you want to punch me out as representative of the police force, let me have it."

"Maybe... Maybe after lunch."

36

Chapter 36

They settled in the lounge room after lunch, large, replete. Ingrid sprawled on the floor with two chapters of assigned reading to do. Casey, unconscious beside her. Liz nestled into the lounge and Robert took a chair.

"That was an excellent lunch," he said, expanding comfortable into the seating.

"It's hard to beat a good steak... You know, morally, I want to be a vegetarian," Liz declared repentant. "But sometimes I crave cooked dead animal. Dead vegetable just doesn't always do it for me."

"Erk," said Ingrid.

"Well, I guess it's hard to overcome thousands of years of predisposition," Robert suggested.

"I... I... never thought of... of a vegetable as dead before," Ingrid said. "I won... wonder if they feel their... death."

"I saw somewhere," Liz mused aloud. "Where a scientist with high frequency sound equipment recorded a plant screaming when it was cut with a knife. But I can't remember if it was legitimate science or an episode of *The Twilight Zone.*"

"I'm going with the latter," Robert said.

"W... What's a latter?" Ingrid asked.

"Let's see, it's a derivative of later," Liz explained patiently. "I said two options, legitimate science experiment, the first earlier statement and *The Twilight Zone*, the second or later statement. Later or latter."

"Okay. Okay, what's, what's a derivative?"

"It's um, like a by product from an original source," Liz explained with slightly less enthusiasm.

"I... I see. What's a, a by product."

Liz looked at Ingrid, saw she was merely amusing herself and let fly with a cushion at her daughter but hit the sleeping dog, who jumped up quickly, escalating straight into game mode, wagging his tail and jumping about.

"Sorry, Casey. Go back to sleep. I was aiming at the woman beside you. Physical abuse of a child to animal abuse in one foul fell swing," Liz said.

Robert laughed.

Ingrid pulled Casey to her and wrestled with him so that he might have a bit of a game for waking up happy. How great to emerge from sleep, even hit rudely by a lounge cushion, smack into to cheerfulness.

"Put the telly on in the background," Liz said. "In case there's a lull. I want to see tomorrow's weather. I feel a gardening spurt coming on."

Ingrid found the remote and aimed it at the box. It flickered to life and there was a surprising close glimpse of male full-frontal nudity above English subtitles.

"Flick the remote. That's just a movie I taped." Liz said quickly and Ingrid flicked obediently and rested the TV on a Ninety Sixties movie. "That's more like it."

"Odd place to pause," Robert said, teasing, smiling.

"The phone rang," Liz said in explanation, throwing off her embarrassment.

"What... What was wrong with his... His thing?" Ingrid asked in her innocence.

"Sorry?" Liz asked

"His... Down there. That man on your movie."

"What? His penis?"

"Yes. Was it... broken?

"Broken? Sorry? I... No, I don't think so. What do you mean? Do you want to turn it back on?"

"No... What? No. I just... It was... "

Robert cleared his throat, "Um, I think perhaps Ingrid hasn't seen a flaccid penis before."

Liz turned slightly red, "Oh," she said. "Oh," she repeated as realisation dropped sharp upon her. "I see. No, it wasn't broken. No. Um, let me see if I can find some information. I think I have a book with pictures that can explain things better than I can. Visual aids, I guess."

Liz left the room in haste. Ingrid and Robert immobile, quiet, both pretended interest in the dull old movie, given no ready conversation and the abrupt end of the earlier talk with Liz's exit.

Casey settled back to sleep and Ingrid flicked pages of her book, trying to find in it her place. A thud was heard from Liz's room then an, "I'm okay."

"You sure? Do, do you need a hand?" called Ingrid.

"No, I found it," Liz called back. "I just need to... " There was another thump from the room. "I'm still O-Kay! Clumsy but, okay."

Robert smiled at Ingrid. She smirked vaguely in his direction.

"I got this for you when you were little," Liz said, entering the room with a picture book in her hand. "But was dithering about the appropriate age to let you read it."

"I think I, I might be old... Enough to read it, n, now."

"I think you might be," Liz agreed, handing Ingrid the book.

"How... How Babies are M... Made," Ingrid read hesitantly.

"You don't have to read it out loud, I kinda know," Liz said.

Ingrid smiled and began reading to herself.

Later, after a few pages there was an, 'Oh!,' of comprehension.

"All has been revealed," Liz said. "I hope the book explained it better than I could," she added.

"I... I didn't realise. Have... Have you ever been... Been 'in love'?"

"I guess. With your dad. Why?"

"It... It just says, when, when two people are 'in love'..."

"Makes it sound like a foreign country. You don't have to be 'in love' to have sex, it just makes it nicer," Liz said.

"Do, do you think you'll be in, 'in love' again?"

"I hope not," Liz answered.

Both Ingrid and Robert looked surprised.

"That was emphatic," Robert said.

"Why n... not?" Ingrid asked.

"It seems to me, and this is a really biased view, that love inevitably leads to pain and loss. I loved your dad, and that was a mess and then I lost him. I loved you and... Well, we all know the pain of that sudden separation."

"But, but you still L... love me?"

"Of course I do!"

"Even though, it, it might lead to loss?"

"Yup. Can't turn it off."

"Do... do you want to turn it off?"

"Nup."

"Okay. So... So what I have learnt, is, men don't always have an up penis and my mother is sc... scared of love."

"Correct on both points, if you'll pardon the expression."

"I think I'll go... go outside and think," Ingrid said, rising from the floor and putting the books on the coffee table. "St... Stretch my, my legs and mind. Come on, Case."

They both left the room in a rush of legs and bounce. Quiet eased in and then filled the space.

"You've gone somewhat subdued," Robert observed aloud, more to say, 'I see,' rather than, 'don't.'

Liz sighed aweary but not defeated. "It's just such a fractured 'hallelujah.' I'm so glad, thankful, she's home, but she's not the Ingrid she was growing into. The child taken is not the adult returned. She could have been... Anything. So much has been laid waste in front of her. By the time she regains her ground... "

"And nobody pays."

"Ingrid does."

"I'm sorry. If I'd looked into your husband's friends deeply, earlier…"

"There can't be recriminations. None of us survive blame. I just fear a little for her after I'm gone."

"But you won't be going anywhere for a while, will you? Besides, Ingrid'll cope. She's survived more than this world could throw at her."

"I know. I just want her path smooth."

"Really, what ever happens to Ingrid from now surely won't be as bad as where she's been."

"Yeah, you're right. Worry, is just my default setting."

"Well, stop it."

"I worry that I can't stop worrying."

"Here, let me get you another wine."

"Are you trying to get me drunk?"

"No, ma'am. I am an officer of the law. I'm just wanting you to have a break from worrying."

"I worry about breaking from worry."

"Shut up."

"Okay."

37

Chapter 37

Again dark shrank the world cold and small, into a vaguely airless box. She felt the walls of the cupboard close, curled as she was with her knees under her chin. Was that fear crawling slick across her skin? That tingle? She brushed her skin, felt something with her hand and was frantic. Bugs? She brushed her bare skin desperately with her hands, hitting the walls, the floor. A whimper, and she quickly pulled the noise back into herself. 'I'll be quiet.' For a long time a cramped nothing. Then panic, then nothing. The dark blanketed over any distractions and brought the precinct of consciousness so uncomfortably near that it turned inward. There was no escape outward. Locked in the apparent safety of the cupboard she was taken again by the troubling prospect of release. Last time... the uneasy recollect of being dragged roughly out from the dark. A problem - free of the oppressive dark was to be hauled into the light of fresh torment. To uncurl her cramped limbs was to open up to... No. I'll be quiet. Lose, lose. Why couldn't she just die? Be dead with her mother? Where was God? Why couldn't she just stop breathing? God? Do you hear me? She heard footsteps. God?

Ingrid awoke in the tempered light of dawn. She lay for a long time, trying to still the part of her that was too alive, and wake the part of her that seemed dead. Time grew from minutes to perhaps hours. Inside, were pieces of shame and an anger at something nameless, perhaps her own self. A slight tremor shook her like a fear. She knew the past had moved further away, behind her, but sometimes it tried to pull her back there, make old damage hurt anew, drag her away from freedom, from safety. There was too much control and not enough control. She felt hurtled from one side to another. Ingrid heard a call for razor blades.

"*Fuck off,*" she murmured to the disquiet.

"Breakfast!" her mother called from the kitchen as if all was very ordinary.

"Coming!" Ingrid called back, chasing this ordinariness, almost tripping in her rush to gain it.

"Good morning, my child," Liz welcomed, as Ingrid entered the kitchen.

"G... good morning, my mum."

"You look a bit peaky. Everything okay?"

"Yes... Peaky?"

"Pale, sickly."

"Why peaky?"

"You got me, kiddo. I've no idea. But are you feeling okay?"

Ingrid shrugged. Who knew?

"Yes. I... I don't know my ankle's a b... bit sore."

"That's no good. Probably the cold. Does the doctor need to see it?"

"I, no. D... don't know."

"He did say if it formed too much scar tissue it could become more painful. Is it lumpy?"

"Yes."

"The plastic surgeon might be able tidy it up, ease the pressure a bit."

"I... I don't want more s... "

"Surgery."

"D... Don't."

"Finish your sentences. I know, sorry. You are a bit tetchy. I guess not everyone can have my sweet nature."

"The... The toaster's sm... smoking."

"Shit!" Liz rushed to the appliance and promptly switched it off at the wall, before the smoke alarm could add its noise to the mix. Casey slid under the table, afraid as Liz ranted. "Stupid piece of electrical crap! Since when does the low setting mean effing charcoal? Why do toasters hate me? Oh. It's on high..."

"Sw... sweet nature..." Ingrid said, rubbing Casey's head with her foot reassuringly, smiling.

"Well, toaster's a bit too easy to knock the dial. I think it's time to get a new one."

"A... another one? You say... Say that about every toaster."

"Well, people take no pride in their appliance manufacture anymore. Everything's so disposable."

Liz upturned the contraption over the bin and let the lumps of smoking black once upon a time bread fall down into the rubbish. "What am I doing?" She wondered aloud, then dropped the recalcitrant toaster ceremoniously in the bin. "Goodbye!.. So, how 'bout you drive us into town and we have breakfast together before you get off to class? Then, purse in hand, I'll wander off and buy another shiny new toaster. But this time I'm not buying generic. I'm going for all the bells and whistles. My toast is not to be trifled with."

"S... Sounds like... like a decent Plan B. Although, I'm not really hungry."

"That's because you were expecting my black toast and iffy jam, not bacon and eggs made by consummate professionals. Go on. Go 'n' have a shower. Take your coffee with you. Time's fleeting."

"Okay. Okay."

Ingrid rose, obedient. She didn't really want to be alone with the inner voices but took her coffee and collected fresh clothes before locking herself in the bathroom. The blades were in a new hiding place, taped to the bottom of the cabinet drawer with a band-aid strip. The interior noise demanded to see them, to see their potential. Ingrid sat on the floor, rocking gently, trying to fight the urge, this injurious compulsion. *No, no!* She felt a familiar troubling anticipation, knew of the inevitable. Lose, lose. *Everything's so disposable.*

A sudden, loud in its silence, release and the damage was done. There was blood. A trade off, a small alleviation, mere muting of noise, a truce of sorts. Ingrid, insentient, looked at her arm, saw that it gaped, knew it needed repair.

"Why won't he leave me alone?" she wanted to ask but found she had no voice. Lost somewhere in the shutdown.

Ingrid dressed as best she could, holding a reddening face washer to the wound. She brushed her hair, cleaned up and stashed the blades in hiding place. Knowing something, some pretence of rightness, would disappear when she left the bathroom, she hesitated, brushed her hair again, rinsed the face washer, drank her cold coffee and cleaned the bloodied sink again.

She wanted to tell her mother of the inside voices. The badgering, insistent noise. She wanted to tell her mother how she'd tried to fight and was beaten, but still she had no voice when she reached Liz. All Ingrid could do was hold her arm in front of her mother, ashamed by the obvious bloody sign of weakness.

Liz paled. 'Peaky,' Ingrid thought.

"Is it bad?" Liz asked, lifting the face washer. "Let's see... Ooo, hon, hospital. Let me get my stuff. Where are the car keys?"

It was early enough that Accident and Emergency was unpeopled and quiet. There was a harshness of artificial lighting in the stark waiting room, adding to Ingrid's desolation.

"Come through," a nurse requested and shepherded them to a treatment room. "So, what happened?" She asked, when they were settled.

Ingrid glanced at Liz.

"She cut herself," Liz answered simply.

"I can see that," the nurse said, "How?"

"With a razor blade."

The nurse raised an eyebrow, "On purpose?" she asked.

Neither Liz nor Ingrid bothered to answer. The nurse busied herself with routine; taking blood pressure, temperature, checking the wound, before she left the room.

"We've got a cutter in twelve," they heard her say with vitriolic loudness. "Better get a psych. consult... As if we weren't busy enough, wasting resources..."

Liz jumped to her feet and headed for the door, incensed and protective.

"It's... it's okay," Ingrid said.

"No, it's not," Liz said. At the doorway, she looked left and right into the hall but could not see the nurse. "Did you get her name?" she asked Ingrid.

Ingrid shook her head. Liz returned to her chair, barely restraining her anger.

"I may just slap that woman, if she comes back," she said.

"They're n... not going to... to lock me up, are they?"

"No, they're not," Liz answered, pushing the words out strong, like a shield over Ingrid. She grabbed her mobile phone from her handbag and pressed buttons, beeping musically as she searched for Doctor Stedman's name in her contacts. "Ah." The phone to her ear, Liz looked over at Ingrid, forlorn on the hospital gurney, shrinking further into herself, holding gauze to her wound. "You won't have to be admitted, I promise. Oh, hello, it's Ingrid Brenner's mother, could I possibly speak to Doctor Stedman?"

A doctor entered the room, smiling a greeting. "Ingrid, is it?"

Ingrid nodded.

"Let's have a look. Okay. That's not too bad."

"Hello, Doctor Stedman, it's Liz Brenner... Fine. Thank you."

"Just let me look closer. This might hurt a tad; I'm just seeing how deep it goes. Okay. Good. Right. We'll find a nurse and get you sewn up. When was your last tetanus shot?"

"... Yes. I'll bring her to your office when we're done here. Thank you. Okay. Goodbye," Liz turned to the doctor examining her daughter. "Ingrid's had a tetanus shot this year."

"Great."

The doctor left and soon returned with the nurse from earlier. Liz flew upright with the force of her own anger, and said, "I'm sorry, nurse, I do hope we're not wasting your precious time. And in future would you kindly use your inside voice when talking to your colleagues? My daughter, the 'cutter' as you so kindly put it, has been through what would probably kill a lesser person. Ingrid's fighting hard to find her place in this world, and she should be treated with the same respect anyone might expect walking into this department with a wound. I'd prefer, doctor, if you wouldn't mind finding another nurse to assist you. We don't mind waiting. We've heard how busy it is."

Both doctor and shocked nurse left the room and Liz flopped into a chair, her hostility spent.

"That... That you s... sounding off?" Ingrid asked.

Liz smiled weakly. "Yes, that's me sounding off."

"I'll... I'll try to remember to always... always use my inside voice inside."

"Your inside voice is another matter entirely."

Ingrid knew not to argue this one.

38

Chapter 38

"What we need to do, is to put some protective strategies in place. You can't keep doing this, Ingrid," Doctor Stedman said. "You have eleven stitches."

"I... I..." Ingrid fell further into her silence, contrite.

"Did you want to kill yourself?"

Ingrid shook her head, "No... Not now," she added.

"But this morning?"

"No. No. But a long t... time ago."

"Before you were rescued?"

Ingrid nodded.

"So, what happened this morning?"

Ingrid shrugged. Sometimes words were not close to enough. She wanted to lay open her insides for Doctor Stedman to see. See and to hear the torment of the noise, including the resounding repetitious urgent voices. To see the pain and consider the vastness of the void where her childhood life should have been. Watch the molten flow of her unexposed long restrained anger look frantic for an exit. Understand the dichotomous clash where the predacious noise met the loud silence of the void. To experience the jagged, raw, damage that the past did every time it thrust its ferocious uninvited way into her nowness. How? How could she explain, her fuckdom? Her perpetual fucking battle. The measureless ache of an inner war veteran? Her fear that she would one day go stark fucking unfixably mad?

"I... hurt," Ingrid said simply.

Doctor Stedman looked at Ingrid for a moment, maybe felt it for a little.

"This," Ingrid said, hitting her chest harshly with a fist. "Is n... not me, yet it is."

The two sat in silence for a mending while.

"I... I am just what... what is left over."

"No. You are much more than that."

Ingrid shook her head in disbelief.

"I see you don't believe me."

"I am... am just re... reaction. R... reflex."

"Are you saying you are without choice?"

"Sometimes. It... It seems. Maybe... M... May," Ingrid gave up in frustration at the difficulty of speech.

"Go on. Take your time."

"Maybe until... until New... Newton's Third Law is... is played out."

"Newton's Third Law, 'for every action, there is an equal and opposite reaction'?"

"Yes."

"Do you think until you've reacted equally to your fifteen years of hell, you'll have no free choice?"

"M... Maybe."

"What if I just say, 'bullshit'?"

"That... That's your... Then... Then why do... do I have no control?"

"You do, you just need to learn to take it, use it. Don't you think there are better coping mechanisms than cutting yourself?"

"Yes. But... But why? Why do I do that? I... I... Fuck!"

"It's okay. Try not to get frustrated. Go on."

"I don't want... want to d... do that, cut. I... I... Shit. It's no b... better than him."

"That's why we need to put some strategies in place. Perpetuating the abuse yourself, is not the answer. Do you know what triggered you this morning?"

"I... I just woke up fucked."

"How long was there between waking up 'fucked' and actually cutting yourself, do you think?"

"I... I don't know. C... couple of hours."

"That's good. You see? We have time between feeling out of control to being out of control, to work on managing the stress."

"B... But I... I... When... when it happened, it h... happened before I knew it... it was over."

"We'll work on that, too. First, we'll teach you to recognise that you might be in distress. When you wake up 'fucked,' see if you can learn to say, 'okay, there might be trouble. Let's do some things that could circumvent the dissociation, so that you can become aware enough to protect your own 'self'."

"E... Easy."

Doctor Stedman smiled.

"I know, it's not easy. Well, growing awareness, sometimes means you do have to 'grow' awareness. Start with a small grain and nurture it a bit," she said.

"G... Ground yourself and a... add compost."

The doctor laughed.

"Nothing to lose. So, next time you wake feeling stressed, if you can, tell yourself it's okay to feel like that, you probably had a bad dream, and then work on de-stressing yourself, not distressing yourself. Be aware that you're in a precarious state and then try to avoid moving yourself into a more dangerous place. Even if it means staying out of the bathroom or not being alone. And yes, it won't be easy. Tell your mum, if you have to. Dob on yourself."

"She... She has enough to worry... about."

"She'll worry more if she thinks you're off somewhere harming yourself."

"I'm... I'm tired."
"I know. It'll get better. It'll get easier. I promise."
"I... I wish..."
"Wish what?"
Ingrid shrugged.
"Oh, bugger. Look at the time. I'm sorry..."
Ingrid stood to leave.
"Please be kind to yourself," the doctor said.

39

Chapter 39
Ingrid decide to still go to classes after her unanticipated appointment with Doctor Stedman.

"Are you sure?" Liz asked, concerned.

"Yes."

"Have you got what you need?"

"Yes."

"Do you want me to call the office and explain?"

"No. M... My mess. I'll tell them something."

"Okay. That's good. What about after? Do you want me to pick you up?"

"No. You go home and play with your new toaster."

"Oh yeah. I forgot about that. Come on. I'll give you a lift up there. Are you sure you're okay?"

"Yes. St... Stop asking me that. Stop worrying."

"It's my job."

"Well, then... t... take the day off."

Ingrid grew hesitant at the door to the classroom. To walk in now, when the lecturer was lecting, if that was the word, all eyes would be on Ingrid. It wasn't as if she could slide in unnoticed, the door was at the front of the classroom. It would be like walking on stage, without the applause. Unfortunately there was still three quarters of an hour before the next class and Ingrid stood dithering at the peek-a-boo window in the door, contemplating the canteen or the library. Some of her classmates looked absolutely bored rigid, a sign that the canteen might be more entertaining. Ingrid made the decision to leave at the same instant that the lecturer noticed her at the door and signalled for her to enter. Just in the nick of time, Ms Brenner. We're about to do a test on quadratic equations. Take your seat."

Ingrid felt so very blessed. To think she could have missed the agony that is algebra exams.

> By using the quadratic formula below, find the zeroes (if they exist)
>
> For each of the following quadratics. Answers may be given in
>
> Decimal or surd form.
>
> $$x = \frac{-b \pm \sqrt{b^2 - 4ac}}{2a}$$

And so, Ingrid's consternation went on.

When she arrived home the first thing she said to Liz was, "If x = 6, wh… why don't they write 6 in the first place?"

"You what now? Are you speaking Mathematics? I don't speak mathematics."

"Stupid algebra test."

"Yuck. You probably need some toast after that. Wouldn't you? Some nice fruit loaf cooked in a brand-new toaster."

"I… I…"

"Sure, you would. Come into the kitchen. Feast your eyes on the brand new beast."

Ingrid followed Liz into the kitchen, followed by Casey.

"Tah dah!" Liz said waving her hand over the machine like an old fashioned game show hostess.

"It's blue. Very blue."

"And shiny."

"But… But does it do good toast?"

"And well you may ask. Sit down and allow me to demonstrate."

Ingrid dropped directly to the floor and began playing with Casey.

"I didn't mean right there," Liz said. "At the table would be the usual option but good enough."

Ingrid grinned. She gave Casey a gentle shove and he bounced back at her with unfettered enthusiasm.

"Mind your stitches," Liz warned, as they wrestled.

"Y... Yes, mum."

"Would you like a drink?"

"No, thanks. You just... mind your toast."

"That's the beauty of the new toaster. It minds itself."

"I'm impressed."

"Ding," said the toaster.

"Isn't that better than the smoke detector going off?" asked Liz, pulling Ingrid's toast from the toaster before slapping some margarine over its surface with a knife.

"It must have cost a bit. I... I want to...give you some money," said Ingrid washing dog off her hands before sitting at the table.

"That's not necessary."

"I... I want to pay... pay my way properly," Ingrid said seriously.

"You pay your way 'properly," Liz said bringing coffees to the kitchen table and sitting down. "And besides, you'll need your money. I was talking to Anne today; her son's decided to stay an extra year in London and wants to sell his car. It's yours for two thousand dollars."

"M... Mine?"

"Yep. To do with what you will. Pretty good, eh?"

"I... I. wow."

"Yes, and don't worry about your carbon footprint, we shall plant trees galore. There's a website."

"I've n... never owned any... anything so big before."

"Yep and it's all yours. All the responsibility for upkeep, repairs, registration, insurance, blah, blah, blah. Leaving me to be chauffeured around in it like Lady Muck, without a care in the world."

"Wh... When does it be... become mine?"

"We can go round after dinner and get the paperwork off Anne. Then to the bank tomorrow, then transfer the rego and voila, it's all yours."

"Wow."

"How's your toast?"

"... Perfect. I... I might ... go out and clean my car after, then have a sh... shower b... before... we go."

"Do me a favour?" Liz asked.

Ingrid nodded her head.

"Give me the blades you have hidden."

This took Ingrid by surprise. Shame smeared over her like a burning injury, but she felt her inner self balk and anger at the idea. There was a mess of thoughts.

"Y... You d... don't t... trust me?"

"I don't trust your demons. Let's just make it a bit harder for them, okay?"

"B... But..."

"But what?"

"I... I... I'm a gr... grown woman."

"I know, hon. But inside, part of you is still a very scared young child trying to find a way out of a most horrendous place."

"I... I," Ingrid was going to argue, but she had to agree. She felt if her mother confiscated the blades and things got too hard to bear anymore, her fast emergency exit would be gone. "Y... You win. I... I give up."

"Don't. Don't give up. Ever."

40

Chapter 40

Before too long Ingrid obtained the license to drive solo. A triumph of woman over machinery. The car, her car, became a sweet obsession. It was a space like she had never known, this strange freedom. Self-reliant movement but still traveling with the cocoon-like security of home. Out in the world, but not in the world.

There was her coffee, steaming in the cup holder. Favorite music through the speakers from her phone. There, her sunglasses sliding about on the dashboard. Here, in its cradle, her mobile phone. In the back seat a spare jumper and her backpack. And, in the glove box, with some shame attached, secreted, sharp, shining blades. Ingrid knew her mother and Doctor Stedman would be very disappointed by this. She had no plans, no need to use them, but a part of her could not give up on the comfort in the knowing. Knowing they were there, knowing there was an outlet, an exit, if things became unbearable. It was as: in emergency break glass.

Casey, his head poked out of the half opened window, the speed flapping his
jowls, like a g-forced grimace, was spraying drool down the glass, happy, going places. A succession of new smells passing in the air. His whole body waggled enjoyment.

There was no room for big thoughts, given that Ingrid's driving skill was still at a level needing a deal of concentration. That was good. Usually, her introspection was like a nest of coat hangers, each thought hooking on another until there was nothing but a gouging grabbing nasty mess. Now, she drove fully present, the moment unencumbered by the past. She was driving it away.

At first Ingrid was planning to stay local, on roads she knew but that world was too small. When she spotted the signs for the freeway she began following the arrows.

"Freeway," she said to Casey, liking the unconstrained sound of it.

Unexpectedly, the freeway was a parking lot. Ingrid had merged nicely into three lanes of tip-to-tail traffic, crawling almost unperceptively towards Sydney or the next exit.

"Balls!" she said.

In what seemed like hours from an elongated tedium place, Ingrid reached an exit and with a number of other impatient drivers, turned off and enjoyed the emancipated breezy increase of speed. Most of the cars diverted onto the old south road leading to Sydney but Ingrid, slightly disoriented, tried to find her way back to the freeway so she could retrace her path northward, home. A sign arrowed to Gosford hinted the direction and Ingrid relaxed back into the groove of untroubled driving and didn't bother consulting maps in her phone.

She turned her music up and felt an unencumbered easiness, driving with a near unconscious competence suited to the lack of traffic. But keeping an edge of readied alertness in case of incident. Rabbits running across the road in front of the car or meteorites crashing to earth. Who knew?

It was a clear Winter's day, without extreme cold and Ingrid began to enjoy this side trip, without having a clue as to where she precisely was. Casey too, bounced about, surprised at cows and other fence-side oddities.

"A cow," Ingrid explained. "A horse."

And then suddenly, thumping like a hit to the chest, Ingrid realised the landscape. There, the rise and fall of the hilltops, so familiar, an old worn photograph etched into her tired memory. She indicated, pulled the car over onto the shoulder and

switched everything off.

Outside, she stood and stared at the terrain, heartbeat erratic, as Casey darted
about peeing on the world. Ingrid wanted to flee. To scream.

She thought this attack a betrayal, a conspiracy hidden in the silence of her
mind. It had used the quiet to manipulate her into what was now obviously an insincere sense of security. This deceitful lull that now made the noise extraordinarily loud and pain filled. He was near. So near.

"Jesus!"

She wanted to cry. The harshness.

Get to the creek, cunt! You fuckin' bled over my new sheets. They're fuckin' Egyptian Cotton. Fifteen hundred thread count. Jesus. Fuck off! Go on! Clean up.
You can't get away with that weight on your chain. Now, fucking out of my sight.

She wanted... something.

"Jesus, Jesus!"

Ingrid paced along the fenceline, backward, forward. Her mind, too, backward, forward. Her hands flapping and banging her thighs. Seeing in the peripheral her old horizon. The visual border of that old narrowed, confined life.

The loudness of the past transgressed explosively, acutely into the surrounds of now. Ingrid raised her hands to her ears. Heard him some more. Felt the need to wee.

No cars. She took her chance, looking at the distinctive hill, she remembered so well, as she relieved herself. The rise and jagged fall of the terrain. Centuries old scars of a land repositioned and weathered. Life had left its gaping wounds. Its marks.

Ingrid went back to the car, fumbled for a Xanax, her mobile phone. She pulled up her sleeves, suddenly in a hot, frightened heat. She pressed buttons Doctor Stedman and was put straight through by her secretary without much need for explanation.

"M... My landscape," she said, looking at the jagged red welts up her
wrists. "I'm... I'm in... In my landscape."

"Sorry?"

"M... My. He's here. In... In my head. F... Fuck! I'll die. I... I..."

"Who? Oh. No, you won't die. Ingrid, where are you? You're scaring me a bit. Slow your breathing. Are you sitting? Ingrid?"

"Y... ah... Yes?"

"Are you sitting?"

"Yeah... I..."

"Breathe. Relax. Okay. Is it safe to close your eyes?"

"Mm."

"Good. Close your eyes. Let's just calm a little bit. Okay, listen to my voice. Now, concentrate on your feet. Feel your toes. Wiggle them. Feel each one individually and then let them drop relaxed. Okay. Now feel your ankles."

"F... Fuck."

"Come on, Ingrid, listen to my voice."

"Ah. No."

"Yes, listen. Tighten your calves. Tight. Okay, now relax them. Tighten
them again. Feel the tightness. Now, relax them. We're relaxing our way toward your busy mind. Feel your knees..."

Eventually, a time came when Ingrid had relaxed out of the panic and was looking at the landscape with the eye of an historian, Casey sleeping beside her, worn from his own explorations.

"The... the farm m... must be so... so near here. I... I stared at that hill... hilltop every day. Fifteen years. Want... Wanting so... much to be there. At the top. Away."

"Well, you don't have to be anywhere you don't want to be anymore.
You are free."

"Yes... Yes. No."

"What do you mean?"

"He... He... rides around in me. L... like I do in th... this car."

"I promise, you'll be free of his pain one day."

"Y... You sure?"

"Sure as I can be. Now, do you think you can get yourself safely home?"

"Y... Yes. As long as there are... are arrows."

"Arrows?"

"S... Signposts. It's okay. I'll put maps on, now."

"I'm pretty vague on that area. Text me when you're safely home, and I'll see you tomorrow at eleven. Okay?"

"Okay. Tha... Thanks."

"You're welcome. Be safe."

Casey woke up, alert, when the car started. Ready for his next big adventure.

Ingrid noted the time on her mobile phone and realised she had lost three hours, before she'd even called Doctor Stedman.

"Bugger," she said. "I'm as crazy as a... what... whatever's crazy. A rab... Rabid dog."

Her own dog was bouncing about excitedly looking through the windscreen, then the side window, trying not to miss anything. Some crazy dogs weren't so bad.

Ingrid's mind was almost silent again. A pure quietness, this, an undamaging calm. She felt the periods of near quiet were becoming happily more frequent. Weren't they? But it was the monstrous ugly loud, in between the silence, that might kill her. She shook her head. No! No bad thoughts. No blades. No. It's home time. She had a home. She had time.

"Let's go home," Ingrid said to Casey.

Soon there was distance between Ingrid and the Peats Ridge area. Between Ingrid and that horrible noise and the dangerous quiet. Even between Ingrid and the blades. Not a distance merely measured in metres or kilometres. Measured in time, maturity and unexpectedly, by lack as well. The fear had dissipated quickly enough to not do the plunge into harsh, heavy nightmare that Ingrid couldn't get out of. This lack, lack of permanent fear was so lightening, A weightless gift.

Yes, there was medications, the doctor, Liz, Casey, but ultimately Ingrid could have let it all become too much. Wallowed, then swallowed, all manner of pills. Ended it before it became overwhelming again. The frequent impacts had been staggering; loud, merciless, panic inducing and death defying. Ingrid at times had prevailed. Had won. It was a victory now. Wasn't it? Being safe in those moments between the noise?

Here she was in Peats Ridge, or its surrounds and she could leave. Ingrid could
go home. Surely, it couldn't get much better than this.

* * *

His name was Didriksson. He is dead.
The End

www.ingramcontent.com/pod-product-compliance
Lightning Source LLC
Chambersburg PA
CBHW070042040426
42333CB00041B/2130